RECONCEPTUALIZING STATE OF EXCEPTION

STUDIES IN LAW, POLITICS, AND SOCIETY

Recent volumes:

Volumes 1–2: Edited by Rita J. Simon

Volume 3: Edited by Steven Spitzer

Volumes 4–9: Edited by Steven Spitzer and Andrew S. Scull

Volumes 10–16: Edited by Susan S. Sibey and Austin Sarat

Volumes 17–33: Edited by Austin Sarat and Patricia Ewick

Volumes 34–77: Edited by Austin Sarat

Volume 78: Edited by Livia Holden and Austin Sarat

Volumes 79–89: Edited by Austin Sarat

EDITORIAL BOARD

Gad Barzilai	*Tel Aviv University, Israel*
Paul Berman	*George Washington University, USA*
Roger Cotterrell	*University of London, UK*
Jennifer Culbert	*Johns Hopkins University, USA*
Eve Darian-Smith	*University of California, Santa Barbara, USA*
David Delaney	*Amherst College, USA*
Florence Dore	*University of North Carolina, USA*
David Engel	*State University of New York at Buffalo, USA*
Anthony Farley	*Albany Law School, USA*
David Garland	*New York University, USA*
Jonathan Goldberg-Hiller	*University of Hawaii, USA*
Laura Gomez	*University of California, Los Angeles, USA*
Piyel Haldar	*University of London, UK*
Thomas Hilbink	*Open Society Institute, USA*
Desmond Manderson	*Australian National University, Australia*
Jennifer Mnookin	*University of Wisconsin, USA*
Laura Beth Nielsen	*American Bar Foundation, USA*
Paul Passavant	*Hobart and William Smith College, USA*
Susan Schmeiser	*University of Connecticut, USA*
Jonathan Simon	*University of California, Berkeley, USA*
Marianna Valverde	*University of Toronto, Canada*
Alison Young	*University of Melbourne, Australia*

STUDIES IN LAW, POLITICS, AND SOCIETY   VOLUME 90

RECONCEPTUALIZING STATE OF EXCEPTION: EUROPEAN LESSONS FROM THE PANDEMIC

Special Issue

EDITED BY

AUSTIN SARAT
Amherst College, USA

GUEST EDITED BY

HANNA-MARI KIVISTÖ
University of Jyväskylä, Finland

GONÇALO MARCELO
University of Coimbra, Portugal

AND

JOSÉ MARÍA ROSALES
University of Málaga, Spain

United Kingdom – North America – Japan
India – Malaysia – China

Emerald Publishing Limited
Emerald Publishing, Floor 5, Northspring, 21-23 Wellington Street, Leeds LS1 4DL.

First edition 2024

Editorial matter and selection © 2024 Austin Sarat.
Individual chapters © 2024 The authors.
Published under exclusive licence by Emerald Publishing Limited.

Reprints and permissions service
Contact: www.copyright.com

No part of this book may be reproduced, stored in a retrieval system, transmitted in any form or by any means electronic, mechanical, photocopying, recording or otherwise without either the prior written permission of the publisher or a licence permitting restricted copying issued in the UK by The Copyright Licencing Agency and in the USA by The Copyright Clearance Center. Any opinions expressed in the chapters are those of the authors. Whilst Emerald makes every effort to ensure the quality and accuracy of its content, Emerald makes no representation implied or otherwise, as to the chapters' suitability and application and disclaims any warranties, express or implied, to their use.

British Library Cataloguing in Publication Data
A catalogue record for this book is available from the British Library

ISBN: 978-1-83608-199-9 (Print)
ISBN: 978-1-83608-198-2 (Online)
ISBN: 978-1-83608-200-2 (Epub)

ISSN: 1059-4337 (Series)

Printed and bound by CPI Group (UK) Ltd, Croydon, CR0 4YY

INVESTOR IN PEOPLE

CONTENTS

List of Contributors ix

Acknowledgements xi

Introduction: Reconceptualizing State of Exception: European Lessons from the Pandemic
Hanna-Mari Kivistö, Gonçalo Marcelo and José María Rosales 1

Chapter 1 A Pandemic That Never Took Place: Discursivity, State of Exception, and Hyperreality
Iraklis Ioannidis 7

Chapter 2 Sequestered Cosmopolitanism: Exception or New Paradigm?
Marin Beroš 35

Chapter 3 Checks and Balances in Times of Pandemics: The Portuguese Example
João Cruz Ribeiro 47

Chapter 4 Finland and the COVID-19 Pandemic – Risks Inherent in a Restrained State of Exception
Tatu Hyttinen and Saila Heinikoski 63

Chapter 5 Constitutionalism and Emergency Rule: Comparing Germany's and Spain's Responses to the COVID-19 Pandemic
José María Rosales 83

LIST OF CONTRIBUTORS

Marin Beroš	Institute of Social Sciences 'Ivo Pilar' – Pula, Republic of Croatia
Saila Heinikoski	Finnish Institute of International Affairs, Finland
Tatu Hyttinen	University of Turku, Finland
Iraklis Ioannidis	Existential Network Scotland, UK
Hanna-Mari Kivistö	University of Jyväskylä, Finland
Gonçalo Marcelo	University of Coimbra, Portugal
João Cruz Ribeiro	University of Minho, Portugal
José María Rosales	University of Málaga, Spain

ACKNOWLEDGEMENTS

In addition to acknowledging the support of COST Action 16211 RECAST to organise the Working Group's workshops, we would like to thank Professor Austin Sarat for his support of this project and the reviewers for their insightful reports.

Gonçalo Marcelo's research is funded by the Foundation for Science and Technology through a research contract (https://doi.org/10.54499/DL57/2016/CP1370/CT0021) and the strategic project of the CECH (UIDB/00196/2020).

INTRODUCTION: RECONCEPTUALIZING STATE OF EXCEPTION: EUROPEAN LESSONS FROM THE PANDEMIC

Hanna-Mari Kivistö[a], Gonçalo Marcelo[b] and José María Rosales[c]

[a]*University of Jyväskylä, Finland*
[b]*University of Coimbra, Portugal*
[c]*University of Málaga, Spain*

On 5 May 2023, the World Health Organization officially declared the end to the global health emergency related to the COVID-19 pandemic, a status that had officially been in place since 30 January 2020.[1] This historical period will certainly be remembered for a number of different reasons, from the very real threat that the new strand of the coronavirus posed to innumerable human lives, not forgetting the strain put on several health systems worldwide, and to the remarkable way in which the unprecedented accelerated development of new vaccines was ultimately able to curb down the pandemic.

Perhaps only now, at a time when the pandemic is behind us, we are beginning to make sense of what happened then. This period, and especially the years between 2020 and 2022, brought several changes to the way people lived and worked, especially during the several lockdowns that were put in place. And it was also a time ripe with reinvigorated intellectual debates and increased polarisation, with a surge in 'vaccine hesitancy' and a number of controversies aiming to cast distrust in science and democratic institutions.

It goes without saying that many of the phenomena of the pandemic bore significant political and legal importance, as governments, parliaments, and other institutions were forced to make decisions in a context of great uncertainty, and often temporarily suspending basic rights such as the right to free movement, with deep implications at national and international levels.

Surely such phenomena call for scholarly analyses and these cannot refrain from assuming an interdisciplinary perspective including some degree of methodological pluralism. From a standpoint of conceptual history, one concept, that of the 'state of exception', seemed to emerge as a backdrop to the several forms of emergency rule that were put into place in different geographies during the pandemic.

Against this background, *Reconceptualizing State of Exception: European Lessons from the Pandemic* is a special issue that puts forward a timely reflection on a major contemporary topic of debate at the intersection between law, political philosophy, and democratic theory. It draws on the cooperative endeavour undertaken by Working Group 3: Concepts, of COST Action CA 16211 *Reappraising Intellectual Debates on Civic Rights and Democracy in Europe*[2] in order to assess the various forms of state of exception/emergency rule brought about by the COVID-19 pandemic from 2020 to 2022, with a focus on European democracies.

Theorised by Carl Schmitt and further developed by Giorgio Agamben and other authors, the concept of state of exception poses a plethora of conceptual, normative, legal, moral, political, and social challenges, which are explored in the issue. Assembling chapters authored by an interdisciplinary team and working with some temporal distance, this issue fills a gap in the theoretical assessment of the current situation, as it aims both to reconceptualise the concepts of state of exception/emergency rule and unpack the implications that the several states of emergency have had to democracy and rights in the context of the COVID-19 pandemic in Europe and its aftermath.

Even though these concepts were already thoroughly examined in constitutional and political debates in the past, in particular during the interwar years in the 20th century, and had seen some significant scholarship develop on them, they acquired a newfound significance with the COVID-19 pandemic from 2020 onwards, to the extent that various forms of emergency rule were put in place, with recourse to varied legal provisions, in different countries. Therefore, reflecting on the significance of these precedents for the future now appears as an inescapable matter.

Furthermore, Europe proves to be a fertile ground for these analyses because it is the locus of a complex interaction between European and national law and decision-making processes, while it also bears witness to a tension between its liberal democratic tradition and the recent appearance of illiberal tendencies that might stand to profit from the challenges to democracy such as those put by emergency rule. As such, making sense of this constellation of concepts and problems by way of an inquiry that is both conceptual and empirically informed is a necessary task that we carry out in this special issue.

Against this backdrop, this collection of chapters is an effort to make sense of these phenomena by bringing together: first, theoretical, conceptual, and normative assessments of the contemporary resurgence of the state of exception/emergency rule amid the COVID-19 pandemic; and second, applied case studies of the plurality of forms such as resurgence assumed in different European countries.

Accordingly, the first pair of chapters consists of two contributions to intellectual debates raised by the legal and political reactions to tackle the pandemic. The first one focusses on how a prolonged emergency affects the very sense of reality, and the second one on how it has transformed the sense of human sociability and its political ideal. Deepening that experience, the following three chapters illustrate with case studies the legal and political intricacies of a number of democratic regimes' responses to the pandemic's political and constitutional challenges. It can thus be argued that, in a way, this issue makes a movement from macro-level theoretical assessments to the concrete analyses of the changes taking place at a national level.

In his chapter, 'A Pandemic That Never Took Place: Discursivity, State of Exception, and Hyperreality', Iraklis Ioannidis reflects on the normalisation of the pandemic through which an exceptional event turns into a long-term condition. Relying on the ideas of Agamben, Baudrillard, and Heidegger, Ioannidis illustrates the biological uses of the term pandemic that denaturalise its own meaning. At stake in this chapter is therefore an analysis of the way in which the response to COVID-19 was itself unprecedented, including in its media coverage and in the implications that it had for citizens in multiple places. This piece thus assesses some of the controversies around COVID-19 and its consequences, and it also contributes to such critical debate on COVID-19 through its critical and even 'provocative' outlook, as the author himself assumes.

Iraklis Ioannidis thus forces us to take a deep look at the very definitions of epidemic and pandemic and, through his semantic analysis and critical look at the alleged 'hyperreality' in which, according to him, COVID-19 inscribed itself, denounces the influence of the 'biological code' in the interpretation of the pandemic and in the legitimation of the measures taken under the aegis of the state of exception. Looking very closely at the several definitions put forward by the World Health Organization, scrutinising the several levels of discursivity produced by the pandemic, and commenting on the way in which, through legal enforcement, the 'right to health' became an obligation with the set of restrictions imposed on citizens, this chapter – whether one agrees with its main claims or not – thus also raises relevant questions concerning the unstable tension between democratic legitimation and technocratic rule, as well as concerns on what the appearance of the 'state of exception' due to COVID-19 might imply for the future.

The second chapter of this issue remains at the level of an overall theoretical assessment of the implications of the COVID-19 pandemic, but this time around by shifting our attention to a more practical and normative level. Indeed, Marin Beroš addresses the moral and political significance of the COVID-19 pandemic by exploring its effects on the ideal of cosmopolitanism. In 'Sequestered Cosmopolitanism: Exception or New Paradigm?', the author ponders over the pandemic's impact on human sociability and commonality, and on the chances of solidarity across borders.

We should not forget that one of the most obvious consequences of the several lockdowns enforced in different countries was the restriction of free movement, including across borders, coupled with the enforcement of 'social distancing'. And it is self-evident how these restrictions run counter to the cosmopolitan ideal of free movement. In this context, Marin Beroš's chapter puts forward a defense of cosmopolitanism, retracing its origins and history, from the Stoics to Seyla Benhabib, and with a strong emphasis on Kant's version of cosmopolitanism, unpacking its defining traits, and assessing the likelihood of its success in the future, in spite of the setbacks caused by the COVID-19 crisis.

Marin Beroš recalls that even before this crisis, cosmopolitanism came to be seen, in Martha Nussbaum's words, as 'a noble but flawed ideal', that is, a moral perspective without much practical impact, in spite of all the developments within the field of international relations and on cosmopolitan democracy of the last few decades. Beroš eventually concludes that we need not abandon cosmopolitan goals in spite of the pandemic, because the cosmopolitan ideal has in the past shown remarkable endurance.

However, these assessments would be mainly theoretical and the issue would be somehow incomplete without the empirically informed analyses of the following case studies in different European geographies. Without any pretention to be exhaustive, this issue aimed at gathering a representative sample of European Union countries, comprising Northern, Central, and Southern European countries. It goes without saying that these countries have constitutions and legal provisions that vary to a great extent but this makes it all the more interesting to bring them together in a comparative perspective. These three case studies depict different, if comparable, experiences of emergency rule in the European Union.

An eloquent case of the endurance of emergency rule is provided by João Cruz Ribeiro. His chapter, 'Checks and Balances in Times of Pandemics: The Portuguese Example', describes in detail the Portuguese constitutional framework concerning the state of emergency and the two periods during the COVID-19 pandemic in which it was implemented, arguing that due to the checks and balances of the Portuguese legal framework, this state of emergency cannot be described as a quintessential case of a 'state of exception'. However, the chapter documents how the Portuguese government kept adopting extraordinary measures even when emergency rule was no longer in force, that way blurring the separation of powers that characterise, temporarily, a state of emergency. As such, and paradoxically, the true 'state of exception' during the COVID-19 pandemic was, or so João Cruz Ribeiro argues, precisely when emergency rule was not formally taking place.

The piece goes on to analyse the several legal arguments put forward between 2020 and 2022 in cases addressed by the Portuguese Administrative Supreme Court and the Constitutional Court, and the apparent contradictions between the two, concluding that there was indeed decisionist behaviour by the government in times of 'apparent normality' and, therefore, that the judicial review somehow proved to be ineffective in these exceptional times in Portugal.

A revealing example of 'a restrained state of exception' is found in Finland's adoption of emergency rule, unlike other countries' 'radical' uses. In their chapter, 'Finland and the COVID-19 Pandemic – Risks Inherent in a Restrained State of Exception', Tatu Hyttinen and Saila Heinikoski show how some provisions from the Finnish Emergency Powers Act were, however, transferred to normal legislation.

Building on the distinction between the concepts of 'radical' and 'restrained state of exception', the chapter discusses the restrictions to fundamental rights put in place in Finland during the pandemic. Drawing upon theoretical insights, the chapter addresses the question of the extent a democratic *Rechtsstaat* can, in times of crisis, compromise its core principles. The analysis shows the resilience of the rule of law in a country, which is also characterised by the highest rule of law index and high trust in authorities and political institutions. Simultaneously, the authors argue that the restrained state of exception can result in restrictions of fundamental rights more easily with the framework of normal legislation and future states of exception, thus bearing risks and implications for the democratic *Rechtsstaat* that will unfold first in the aftermath of the COVID-19 pandemic.

This special issue ends with a comparative perspective between the cases of Germany and Spain, which are also examples of moderate cases of emergency rule. In his chapter, 'Constitutionalism and Emergency Rule: Comparing Germany's and Spain's Responses to the COVID-19 Pandemic', José María Rosales argues that, in spite of their many legal similarities, their respective governments' decisions between 2020 and 2022 disclose a very different understanding of emergency rule's constitutional gravity.

More specifically, Rosales argues that the decision-making strategies in this period leaned towards a greater centralisation in Germany and a stronger decentralisation in Spain, claiming that this partially reflects different constitutional cultures. Namely, the German parliamentary culture proved to be more resilient, with the *Bundestag* maintaining its normal course, while the Spanish Congress of Deputies remained almost idle for several months.

José Maria Rosales claims that emergency rule is a testing field for the resilience of the constitutional order, and that the success of a democratic regime is also measured by the vitality of its parliament. As such, and drawing parallels from the interwar period of the 20th century, the chapter concludes that 'the longer the recourse to emergency rule, the more difficult it becomes to get back to the normal functioning of a constitutional democracy'.

This and other lessons from the pandemic and its experience with emergency rule prove that, also in legal and constitutional terms, these were exceptional times, likely with a lot of legal and political implications for the future. Drawing insights from different scholarly perspectives and combining the analysis of intellectual debates with empirical case studies, this collection aims to contribute to analysing these recent developments, their consequences, and the lessons that can be drawn from legal, political, and philosophical perspectives.

NOTES

1. https://www.who.int/news/item/05-05-2023-statement-on-the-fifteenth-meeting-of-the-international-health-regulations-(2005)-emergency-committee-regarding-the-coronavirus-disease-(COVID-19)-pandemic
2. See https://www.uma.es/costactionrecast.

CHAPTER 1

A PANDEMIC THAT NEVER TOOK PLACE: DISCURSIVITY, STATE OF EXCEPTION, AND HYPERREALITY

Iraklis Ioannidis

Communications Faculty, SHS/ Existential Network Scotland, UK

ABSTRACT

We have come to a point where the common way to characterise what is taking place presently, or, better yet, for the past almost two years, is with the term 'pandemic'. The task of this chapter is to bring to awareness certain critical reflections with the hope of disturbing the normalised discourse which excepts the authentic meaning of pandemic, a meaning which affects the totality of the human existence. Following the thoughts of Agamben, Baudrillard, and Heidegger, the hypothesis that this chapter is advancing revolves around the idea that the term 'pandemic' has been appropriated by biological thinking excepting its authentic meaning, that is, the ultimate reality of the human existence which is death.

Keywords: COVID-19; state of exception; hyperreality; pandemic; death

INTRODUCTION

We have come to a point where the common way to characterise what is taking place presently, or, better yet, for the past almost two years, is with the term 'pandemic':[1] 'We are/were in a pandemic'. Such phrases, along with their variations, have been normalised in everyday discourse. Normalised here means becoming a rule like a kind of implicit regulation which everyone has to follow. Suggesting, like the title of this chapter, that a pandemic did not take place can range from ludicrous or scandalous, to dangerous or, even blasphemous – if one takes (medical) science as a religion. Yet, a critical consideration of what has been taking place could reveal that what has been, discursively and mass-mediately, constituted and propagated *as a pandemic is not (a) pandemic*. Unless one is religiously adhering to the medical sense forced onto the term 'pandemic', a force which excepts its authentic sense, then what has been taking place is not (a) pandemic. It is a pandemic which never took place. Instead, what took place is a simulation of a pandemic which excepts the ultimate reality of the human condition: the only authentic pandemic that takes place which is death.

This chapter offers a critical consideration of what took place. Before initiating this exploration, a clarification of what constitutes 'critical', in this chapter, is required. 'Critical' today is being conceptualised and practised either as judging, destroying, or deconstructing. 'Critical' is usually thought either in an Aristotelian–Hegelian way – identifying thesis, antithesis, and then providing a synthesis – or in Kantian way as a critique. Derrida (2008) for instance writes:

> All the same, and in spite of appearances, deconstruction is neither an analysis nor a critique, ... No more is it a critique, in a general sense or in a Kantian sense. The instance of krinein or krisis (decision, choice, judgment, discernment) is itself, as is all the apparatus of transcendental critique, one of the essential 'themes' or 'objects' of deconstruction. (p. 4)

What matters in being critical is this *instance of krinein* or *krisis/crisis*. It seems as if deconstruction presupposes critique, but the reverse is not necessary. Derrida's (2008) deconstruction, flowing from Heidegger's *destruction*, which in turn flows from Nietzsche's hammer, equates critique with being critical; and all of that with decision: 'A critical question – the question of critique, in other words, of decision' (p. 217). Yet, as Derrida avows in a different paper, when an 'interpretation is more "critical"', then 'it *suspends* the naïve ontology' (p. 260). Before any decision, there is suspension, a de-*cision*, which means to break, to crack in the way a bolt of lightning cracks the dark as Heraclitus used to say. The *instance of krinein* or *krisis/crisis* is, thus, this break of what is. The offering of this chapter, then, is critical in the sense of suspending the naïve ontology which holds that a pandemic took place.

Unfortunately, critical thinking is not thought in this way today due to its own crisis. But this time, the crisis is medical. That is, the medical thinking has absorbed and pushed aside the authentic possibility of our critical being or our being critical. In one of his interventions, Agamben (2021) writes:

> 'Krisis' was originally a medical concept which designated, in the Hippocratic corpus of texts, the moment when the doctor decided whether the patient would be able to survive the disease. (p. 38)

Astonishingly, Agamben accepts that *krisis* was originally a medical concept. Yet, a look at the so-called Pre-Socratics reveals effortlessly that the Hippocratic *krisis* was not discursively widespread since *krisis* meant, first and foremost, to separate and to distinguish at the same time. Melissus from Samos writes:

κρίσιν δὲ ταύτην χρὴ ποιήσασθαι τοῦ πλέω καὶ τοῦ μὴ πλέω· εἰ μὲν οὖν χωρεῖ τι ἢ εἰσδέχεται, οὐ πλέων.
(in Harriman, 2019, p. 218)

As Melissus writes, *krisis* is the result of poesis (ποιήσασθαι); the result of a power which separates and unites at the same time. If we look at the medical use of the term *krisis* presently, the paradoxical element of either/or is still there yet consumed in a biological reference. Today, to be in a critical condition may bring to mind a state between life and death; perhaps in the emergency room (ER) or in a coma, just like many people were found due to COVID-19. To be in a critical condition is to be in a state of indeterminacy: neither alive nor dead but somewhere in between. In the Hippocratic use of the term, the element of indeterminacy is kept since the doctor decided *whether/or* but through the medical use the meaning of a power which separates and unites at the same time is consumed in/by the doctor's decision. Yet, crisis/krisis is neither decision nor judgement. These are *the effects of crisis*. Crisis/krisis as a power that separates and unites at the same time is found in the *cision* of de-*cision* which does not have meaning but allows for the meaning of decision to come to be.

Before proceeding critically, a note on the semantic play of breaking the 'decision' is required. This semantic play, along with the rest of the play of words which follows in this critical undertaking, will certainly create uneasiness. The semantic play, as all plays, plays two parts. First, it breaks the formality and seriousness of the normativity of discursive uses – as such, it will help us break the normativity of 'pandemic' which is used to characterise what has been taking place for the past two years. Second, semantic play allows for possibilities of meaning to come about. Playing breaks the rules of the norm and creates a crisis. Without such a crisis there cannot be a critical undertaking. Our being critical or our critical being is realised by creating a rupture in norms. Playing is, thus, a key philosophical method for delivering our promise.

Doing philosophy in the normalised platonic way demands arguments about what is the case. A critical undertaking offers crises, it does not offer arguments. Being critical goes beyond argumentation in the sense of convincing about that which is the case. As such, this chapter does not offer any arguments. Its philosophical values rest on its being critical. Essentially, as it will become clear in the next section, our undertaking as critical is to enact a state of exception in a discourse which excepts death, the ultimate reality of human existence which is pandemic. There is, thus, no argument, but a crisis to what is followed uncritically, that is, the medical use of 'pandemic'.

To follow uncritically is also to follow religiously. A crisis in religious thinking is profanity. Agamben (2007) uses the term profanation to explain the power of arresting the religious thinking which excludes other, new ways of thinking to come about. To be profane means to allow the new and the other, the different, to be possible. A profanation amounts to creating an exception to what is religiously taken in. We have been religiously using the term 'pandemic' by having been taken in by its medical sense. Such sense, which used to be a possibility of sense, is now becoming a normative sense. It is this sense to which we are being critical in this chapter. To enact such a state of exception, we undertake a crack in what is being normalised in contemporary discourse as (a) pandemic. To resume being critical, we first need to crack (on with) our contemporary discursive use of pandemic.

We will first start with Agamben's interventions during the past two years on the so-called 'pandemic' in order to offer a possible interpretation of what he calls the state of exception. Our reading of Agamben, or any other philosopher to whom we appeal for help, is one of the possible readings and by no means do we offer it as orthodoxy. After Gadamer's and Derrida's hermeneutic work it would be at least philosophically futile to entertain the idea of a 'proper' reading of a text. Our reading reveals that Agamben's use of the syntagma 'state of exception' starts by following Schmitt, yet in his later works, it takes more of an existential nuance which allows us to employ it here in order to articulate our hypothesis.

Following Agamben's interventions, we shall explore 'pandemic' and trace how the state of exception in the political domain is, perhaps, a concomitant of a state of exception on the existential level. To articulate this hypothesis, we rely on Heidegger whose philosophical vocabulary will allow us to rephrase something which is neither new nor extraordinary. It is old, banal, and forgotten. Yet, this forgetfulness makes it shocking and scandalous when it resurfaces: The only pandemic is the destiny of human existence which is death. The current 'pandemic' which refers to the spread of a 'deadly' virus is but a simulation of 'pandemic' based on a medical code whose main effect is to level down what is always already taking place pandemically.

What is taking place with the phenomenon coded COVID-19 is a simulation of 'pandemic'; simulation means *as if*: as if there is something pandemic. The idea of simulation requires the help of Baudrillard's critical work, and so does the illumination of the provocative title 'A pandemic which never took place'. This title is inspired by Baudrillard's work on the Gulf War. Baudrillard's critical intervention with respect to that war was that what was taking place in the Gulf War had nothing to do with war insofar as the latter, in its historical occurrences, required human bodies confronting each other on the battlefield. What was taking place in the Gulf War was *as if* there was a war.

Baudrillard will also help us illuminate the 'how' of this simulation. This simulation is not something that we experience passively. Having been *seduced* by the medical code, this simulation is lived uncritically since it offers an alternative to facing our authentic pandemic which is death.

TOWARDS AGAMBEN'S STATE OF EXCEPTION

Almost a year ago, on 26 February 2020, Giorgio Agamben published a radical reflection on the so-called coronavirus ('L'invenzione di un'epidemia').[2] Among other things, Agamben argued that a biological issue (the virus) has been constituted as creating a state of emergency that threatens the biological public safety. The constitution of the effects of the virus as an emergency has, in turn, been constituted as necessitating a series of measures which restricted citizens' possibilities of action previously deemed lawful or legal: 'the limitations of freedom imposed by governments are accepted in the name of a desire for safety that was created by the same governments that are now intervening to satisfy it' (Agamben, 2021, p. 2). Agamben has never argued that there has not been an outbreak of a virus. Instead, what he argues is that the biological phenomenon is being exploited politically in order to enforce particular measures against individual liberties, measures which supposedly would prevent the negative effects of the biological phenomenon from taking place. Specifically, 'we are dealing with a growing tendency to trigger a state of exception as the standard paradigm of governance' (p. 1).

One way to approach what Agamben means with the syntagma 'state of exception' is to refer to his work on Schmitt.[3] In *Dictatorship*, Schmitt (2013) tries to illuminate the concept by going through its various uses in political theory. The state of exception quite literally refers to the suspension or temporary abolition of a normal political process which in the West, at least, has been the democratic process. In cases of rebellions, (civil) wars, and dictatorships, there is always a suspension of the political process and, as Schmitt observes, 'whoever rules over the state of exception therefore rules over the state, because he decides when this state should emerge and what means are necessary' (p. 14). The reason for suspension is supposedly the well-being or the security of the people of the state. Whoever rules over the state of exception is sovereign in the full sense of the term. With Schmitt, we have the first philosophical attempt to explain sovereignty through the state of exception.

Yet, the state of exception is not the same in all cases. For instance, Schmitt (2013) carefully distinguishes between a dictatorship which tries to abolish the juridical process in order to establish a new one and a dictatorship which tries to protect it. Having made this distinction, the state of exception is reserved for the latter form as the exceptional measures that are required in order to secure the safety of the political norm or constitution. Whereas in *Dictatorship*, the state of exception is clarified through the figure of dictatorship, in his subsequent work, *Political Theology*, the state of exception will be approached through the suspension of the juridical process, that is, the suspension of the law. Here, the concept of decision becomes key. As Ward (2021) explains, '[t]he power to make the determinative "decision", to reshape "juridical regulation" in the critical moment, thus defines sovereignty in "absolute purity"' (p. 193).

However, and many exegetes of Schmitt miss this point, the sovereign is not only the one who suspends the law but also the one who decides that *there is a necessity* to suspend it. Here, the decision takes the form of judgement. *Just before the decision of the suspension of the law and the passing into the state of exception, there is another decision which makes it*

> [...] clear who the sovereign is. He decides whether there is an extreme emergency as well as what must be done to eliminate it. Although he stands outside the normally valid legal system, he nevertheless belongs to it, for it is he who must decide whether the constitution needs to be suspended in its entirety. (Schmitt, 1985, p. 60)

The sovereign stands outside of the valid legal system because they can suspend it, yet the sovereign, at the same time, belongs to it because the very possibility of suspension has been inscribed within it, that is to say, in this context, quite literally, it has been authorised in cases of *emergency* or *necessity*.[4] Such cases which threaten the security of the political system, for whatever reason, allow for the possibility of its suspension. Yet, as Agamben carefully observes, the decision on whether something constitutes an emergency or a necessity cannot be derived legally or objectively. The decision on whether there is an emergency or necessity is a subjective judgement and as such anomic – it cannot be derived by law nor emerge objectively or factually, supposing that there is such a thing. Equally, the decision to exit the emergency where the law is to be reactivated is again subjective and, thus, equally anomic, 'Not only does necessity ultimately come down to a decision, but that on which it decides is, in truth, something undecidable in fact and law' (Agamben, 2005, p. 35).

It is at this point that the state of exception for Agamben (2005) takes a different meaning than that of Schmitt. The state of exception is no longer *just* (the) suspension of the juridical order.

> In the decision on the state of exception, the norm is suspended or even annulled; but what is at issue in this suspension is, once again, the creation of a situation that makes the application of the norm possible .... That is, the state of exception separates the norm from its application in order to make its application possible. It introduces a zone of anomie into the law in order to make the effective regulation [normazione] of the real possible. (p. 36)

If subjective judgement is anomic, a living law as decision, it still has a force of either suspending or applying the law. If nomos is the norm as juridical law, then its application or suspension resides outside its (normative) force. The state of exception, then, is the threshold between the norm as law and the possibility of its application as force. The possibility of separating law and its application is the state of exception as zone of *undecidability*; forceful suspension and suspended force: pure crisis.

> The state of exception is the device that must ultimately articulate and hold together the two aspects of the juridico-political machine by instituting a threshold of *undecidability* between anomie and nomos, between life and law. (p. 86, emphasis added)

The state of exception as the threshold between anomie/life and nomos/law can thus be conceptualised as the limit of both, 'effective though fictional' (p. 86): the horizon as the limiting point of each, the crack as the possibility of their separation, pure crisis.

Another element that is importantly clarified by Agamben when it comes to the state of exception is its atemporality.

> There are [sic.] not first life as a natural biological given and then their implication in law through the state of exception. On the contrary, the very possibility of distinguishing life and law, anomie and nomos, coincides with their articulation in the biopolitical machine. Bare life is a product of the machine and not something that preexists it, just as law has no court in nature or in the divine mind. (p. 88)

To understand the atemporality of the state of exception we need to digress by suspending our normalised linear way of thinking and think in the logic of the event. Our normalised linear way of thinking is in a sense nihilistic as it is binary. It excludes the middle term by being grounded on the principle of non-contradiction. The event, as something taking place, requires suspension of this thinking. A serious attempt is required here to be critical and suspend it;

otherwise, we will end up reading the state of exception linearly, as Finlayson (2010) does, and miss how the state of exception takes place according to Agamben. To understand this taking place, we first need to go back to Heraclitus.

In what has been designated as fragment 5, Heraclitus (2010, DK 5) says: συλλάψιες·ὅλα καὶ οὐχ ὅλα, συμφερόμενον διαφερόμενον, συνᾷδον διᾷδον καὶ ἐκ πάντων ἓν καὶ ἐξ ἑνὸς πάντα. In this fragment, Heraclitus, in his cryptic way, tells us how *from the one many* and *from the many the one*. This one too many structure takes place without *having taken* place. If it had taken place, then it would have finished; as an event, it is taking place and in that taking place there is no beginning or end.[5] In the one too many structure, we do not have beginning or end but possibility, suspension, exchange, analogy, reversal, and synchrony/simultaneity:

(A) The one suspends itself and exchanges itself into an equivalent or an analogy of many.
(B) The many suspend themselves and exchange themselves into an equivalent or an analogy of one.

A and B are taking place at the same time – they do not coincide, however. The one and many as possibilities are *incidental* not coincidental. The incident is a happening, a taking place. A taking place, as long as it takes place, does not have a beginning or end. As Plato observed a long time ago, you cannot have a beginning with no end. An end is already foreclosed in a beginning no matter how a beginning is conceptualised.

When Heidegger (1962) tries to explain Being, he employs this structure of the taking place of taking place without beginning or end. All around us, we see beings, many particular things. All these particulars taken together cannot make a totality of Being. What happens, what is taking place, is that Being (one) suspends and manifests itself through beings (many). Yet, by revealing itself through something other than it is, other beings, it conceals and unconceals itself at the same time as it actually is, that is, one. For this to happen, Being appropriates or enowns itself. In this enowning, Being reveals itself by withdrawing itself as Being, it relieves itself into (a manifestation of) beings which equally both conceal and unconceal Being. In other words, Being *defers* itself in being what it is, as Being, and turns itself into something other than it is, something different. Being is not the many beings but Being *exemplifies* itself through beings.[6] However, this is not linear. It is not first Being and then beings. As an event, Being's one too many structure is *now* taking place; it has not taken place otherwise it would have been finished or it would have not been.

For Heidegger (1998), human existence is able to be attuned to this process of the taking place of Being precisely because it is there, it stands in that threshold where the taking place is taking place. That threshold is no thing, nothing in particular, but there, where Being into being takes place. But this taking place is neither chronological nor topical. It is meta-physical, beyond the physical, *au-dela* the physical if physical is meant to relate to material sensing. As a threshold, in this event of Being, human existence is in crisis: neither just being; just a body, like all other bodies nor just ideal, like Being; human existence, standing there, in that threshold, is what Heidegger calls ek-static, both belonging and not belonging to what is happening there. Just like in being a witness, human existence is and is not part of this event and can make a telling, that is, logos, of this taking place.[7]

In other words, human existence is itself *excepted* from Being by *being there* in that threshold of indeterminacy. The latter is the limiting point of two anti-nomical forces Being/beings which is a zone of pure violence. Violence etymologically is authentically traced to the 'via' or 'βία' from which we get authentic life, 'vie', 'βίος'. Human existence is found in that passage, abandoned in that zone of indistinction, of violence, of ek-stacy. Human existence can then express both these forces of Being and being, as *being* abandoned *there*. It is precisely because human existence is excepted from the totality that it can have a conceptualisation of it by being both universal (Being) and particular (being).[8] Human existence experiences this event by thinking, which, if it is thinking, it is necessarily critical as an expression of being there, in being attuned to this crisis. Thinking as an expression of this crisis, that is, critical, is questioning rather than reasoning as calculating.[9]

Before we proceed, we note that it is becoming evident how the ek-static condition of the human beings runs parallel with the ek-static structure of the sovereign who can call for the state of exception as conceptualised by Schmitt. Agamben (2005) writes:

> *Being-outside, and yet belonging*: this is the topological structure of the state of exception, and only because the sovereign, who decides on the exception, is, in truth, logically *defined in his being by the exception*, can he too be defined by the oxymoron ecstasy-belonging. (p. 35, second emphasis added)

Just as the being of sovereignty is an expression of this ek-static structure so is language:

> Once again, the analogy with language is illuminating: In the relation between the general and the particular (and all the more so in the case of the application of a juridical norm), it is not only a logical subsumption that is at issue, but first and foremost the passage from a generic proposition endowed with a merely virtual reference to a concrete reference to a segment of reality (that is, nothing less than the question of the actual relation between language and world). (p. 39)

The passage as threshold, as pure mediality, is where or what Agamben reconceptualises as the state of exception.

For Agamben (2005), the polis is equally an expression of that threshold. We have been accustomed to thinking in a linear fashion *as if* human existence evolves from animal to being human. The evolutionary narrative, attractive or 'scientifically proven' as it might deemed to be, has accustomed us to thinking as if we are first animals and then evolve into political and rational animals as Aristotle supposedly wrote. However, Agamben's reading of Aristotle shows that human existence is political not because we evolve, but because human existence expresses itself creatively out of the violence, out of the exceptional standing that it has: the polis is not just a collection of individuals but the creative discharge of human existence where the many come to be one – and the reverse; one too many become one polis both as material and ideal, physical and cultural.

The polis, as an expression of human existence as it is, is an event. As we mentioned earlier, an event is taking place and *has not taken* place. That is why there is no beginning or end when it comes to the polis. For Agamben (2005), the possibility for human existence to realise its condition within the polis, that is, of making the distinction that it is both material and ideal, makes human existence on the verge of being dissolved – 'the very possibility of distinguishing life and law, anomie and nomos, coincides with their articulation in the biopolitical machine' (p. 87). This is why the state of exception is pure crisis.

Pure crisis, however, is beyond the dialectic of good and bad. Authentic human praxis for Agamben (2005) springs from such critical state. Politics comes from such a critical state when the antinomical forces are creatively expressed in a harmonised action, gracefully, without one appropriating the other. A polis is an expression of the violence of the general and the particular. Authentic political expression comes when the general/particular, life/law, public/private are discharged through 'the state of exception in which they are bound and blurred together' (p. 86); when they are de-*cided* through a juridico-political order without being in coincidence, without being coin-*cided*. Their coincidence suggests a pure state of exception where both are consumed by no-thing in particular – since the ontology of the exception is no-thing in particular. Their coincidence is a state of nihilism. In such a state, they are both included in their exclusion and excluded in their inclusion, absolute crisis. Things get worse when these antinomical forces 'tend to coincide in a single person' and thus the 'juridico-political system transforms itself into a killing machine' (p. 86).

STATE OF EXCEPTION AND COVID-19

In the past two years, the COVID-19 phenomenon has been the pretext for triggering such a state of exception. The exceptional measures which were taken to secure public health came at the expense of political freedoms. The way governments acted with respect to dealing with the effects of the biological phenomenon has been non-democratic. Specifically, the restrictions were issued through acts and decrees which have the force of law without themselves being legal, insofar as law in modern democracies is produced through a legislative parliamentary process overseen by a judicial power. Yet, they are legal insofar as governments have included in their constitutions the potentiality of such suspension in cases of emergency. Such a phenomenon of a provisional abolition of the 'normal' governing process, in our case today, the democratic process, that is, the distinction among the legislative, executive, and judicial powers, constitutes one of the essential characteristics of the 'state of exception'. The legislative and judicial powers, as if dissolved, are consumed by the executive; they are excepted, included in their exclusion. They are not abolished but abandoned.

Seen individually, that is, isolated and out of historical context, most people were convinced that the spread of the virus was unprecedented and that the measures taken were required in order to overcome the threats that it posited – even if that meant to sacrifice their freedom. That is, that the state of exception was indeed quite literally exceptional. One of Agamben's (2005) arguments derived from his work on Schmitt and his genealogical studies, is that the calling of the state of exception is no more exceptional but has become the norm, the rule. In *The State of Exception*, Agamben (2005) devotes almost 20 pages (pp. 5–17) to demonstrate how we have been living in an ongoing state of emergency which is being exploited to suspend political freedoms. Be it the pretext of war (WWI, WWII, and Cold War) or terrorism, the West has been in a constant state of exception derived from the calling of emergent threats to the security of the states. The state of exception has been normalised. Now that terrorism is not an issue, another pretext must be used in order to justify the sovereign decision of suspending the law and of creating this legal anomie. The biological phenomenon coded COVID-19 fitted perfectly as a reason for maintaining the ongoing state of exception. The biological safety falls under the category of political security which allows the state of exception to be justifiably perpetuated: 'Governments that deploy the security paradigm do not necessarily produce the state of exception, but they exploit it and direct it once it occurs' (p. 11) – see also Ward's (2021) analysis on how the political steps to regulate COVID-19 in the UK are (bio)politically analogous to those of the regulation of prostitution in the previous century.

Back in the days of the spread of the H1N1 virus, the World Health Organization (WHO) was trying to trigger a similar crisis, but such crisis never occurred. As Cindy Patton (2011) carefully observes, the 'WHO's incomplete sovereignty was threatened when the European Council ... and several member countries refused to accept the WHO's designation of pandemic' (p. 108). What happened in the case of the virus coded COVID-19? Was it really that unprecedented? No matter the attempt to lay down possible criteria of comparison, the idea that COVID-19 was the worst plague when compared to others, will remain purely speculative. Throughout the many plagues that have occurred in history, Moote and Moote (2004) note that each generation thinks that their plague was worse than the previous ones. Nietzsche (1996), in a prophetic way, had paid particular attention to such workings of vanity. Just like every generation thinks it is better or more progressed than the previous ones by supposedly knowing better, so it 'knows' that the tragedies that befall on it are more tragic than the previous ones. An unprecedented pandemic never took place.

Let us look at it differently. The democratically elected governments are supposed to represent the interests of the majority. Yet, the representation of these governments had never included what would be the plan in case of a biological phenomenon which could threaten the biological public safety. The measures taken were all decrees based on a particular constitution of the biological phenomenon. The governments were supposedly consulted by the scientific community, yet the very scientific community has been fragmented in terms of the constitution of the severity of the phenomenon.[10] Scientists have disagreed both in terms of the severity of the phenomenon and, also, in terms of the ways to treat its effects. A pandemic has not taken place in the full sense of the term 'scientifically'.

But even if there were a consistently unified and coherent constitution of the phenomenon, it no way logically follows how it should be treated. Logically speaking, as Hume (1896) demonstrated long time ago, the ought can never be derived from the is. There is an outbreak of a virus. Indeed there is one, yet how to deal with this cannot be derived from what is. This may sound strange, but logically it is not. For instance, there are individuals who take a Nietzschean approach to life, or, better yet, they take an approach which Nietzsche calls Hellenic. What does this mean? Suppose I'm not feeling well and I feel I have a fever. Instead of swallowing chemicals, I go running and I try to overcome what affects me in a non-chemical way. If it won't kill me, it will make me stronger. Treating a biological condition is in no way a one-way street. There is a virus that affects us. The way to treat it will ultimately depend on the orientation that one has about their existence. In the case of a polis, treating something that affects it, is first and foremost political. As Agamben (2021) explains, in our modern (bourgeois) democracy, we used to entertain such options since health was supposed to be a right. Yet, the way the virus has been dealt with presently has turned this right dialectically into a legal obligation. The exception in this case runs in the obligation consuming the right. We are obligated to exercise our right to be healthy.

Even more, this obligation is not only about being healthy but, also, about being healthy in a particular way *excepting* all other possibilities and, all the more so, the dialogue of what other possibilities would have to offer. Going back to Heidegger (1998), the exception of possibilities in dialogue, that is, one appropriating the many without allowing them to be, comes as a perfect nihilism. 'Nihilism is consummated when it has seized all subsisting resources and appears wherever nothing can assert itself as an exception any more, insofar as such nihilism has become our normal condition' (p. 296). What is nihilated here is indeed the political insofar as the latter is founded on the possibility of deliberation. Deliberation has been utterly excepted when it comes to treating the outbreak of the virus. What has been seized and ceased here is both the scientific deliberation, insofar as there were scientists who were silenced for holding a different opinion about the virus, and the possibilities of treating the virus in ways other than restricting freedoms.

Agamben (2021) argues that this virus came as the perfect pretext in order to maintain the state of exception that has become the norm ever since WWI. This argument gains a lot of support when we look again, closely this time, at Paton's analysis where it is clear that in the previous outbreak of H1N1, governments retained their sovereignty and did not follow the suggestions of the WHO in treating that outbreak as a pandemic in the biological sense. In the previous outbreak, deliberation took place since the state of exception had been triggered through other pretexts like war and terrorism. The phenomenon coded COVID-19 was thus politically exploited to further a normalised political form of governance. For Agamben (2021) 'it is irrelevant whether [the pandemic] is real or simulated' (p. i). What matters is that it is politically exploited in order to trigger and maintain the state of exception:

> More serious epidemics have happened in the past, but nobody ever dared declare for that reason a state of emergency which keeps us from moving, like the present one does. People have become so used to living in a state of perennial crisis and emergency that they seem not to realise that their lives have been reduced to a purely biological state. Life is losing not only its social and political dimensions, but also its human and affective ones. A society which exists in a constant state of emergency cannot be free. We live in a society that has sacrificed freedom 'for security reasons', and has hence condemned itself to living in a perpetual state of fear and insecurity. (pp. 4–5)

The security reasons to which Agamben refers in this passage are not political. He refers to the primacy of maintaining natural life, bare life as he calls it, or, what in normalised discourse we call biological, over any kind of political life which, as we saw, is the expression of both nature and culture, body and mind. The recent 'pandemic' is an attempt to consummate the state of exception where the biological consumes the social and political dimensions of life. In the quotation above, Agamben argues that *people have become so used to living in a state of perennial crisis and emergency that they seem not to realise that their lives have been reduced to a purely biological state.* One way to understand this 'being used to' is through our discursive practices. To trace and track this exceptional phenomenon, we, thus, need to play with semantics.

EPIDEMIC, PANDEMIC, AND THE BIOLOGICAL EXCEPTION(S)

One way to understand that we are in a state of exception where natural/physical life has consumed the social and political aspects of human life is to look at the term 'biological'. The way we use 'biological' today is a clear expression of the state of exception. This term has been normalised in its reference by excluding the distinction that existed in ancient times and it has become 'the secularized term for naked life' (Coulter, 2005, p. 4). Agamben (2000), in his many close readings of Aristotle, tries to revive the distinction according to which *zoe* refers 'to the simple fact of living common to all living things' and *bios* which 'signified the form or manner of living peculiar to a single individual or group' (p. 2). Finlayson (2010) tries to argue against Agamben's reading 'that the distinction between *zoe* and *bios* was *pandemic* in the ancient Greek language' (p. 106; second emphasis added). The fact that the distinction still exists somehow in the modern Greek language is more than adequate evidentiary support for Agamben's attempt to show that biology as referring to bare life, and thus becoming a synonym for zoology, would be incomprehensible in ancient times. Today, the coincidence of zoology and biology where both refer to bare/naked life is proof that we are living in what he, following Foucault, calls biopolitics. That is, a form of life which is consumed or exhausted in securing and controlling *zoe* while sacrificing anything else. *Bios* is now consumed in *zoe*. The manner of living is fully exhausted in securing bare life by excepting its other possibilities. This is an asthenic life, a deceased bios or a life where authentic bios has been dis-abled, dis-eased.[11]

The discursive use of 'pandemic' in order to come to terms with the natural phenomenon coded COVID-19 constitutes another expression of the state of exception that we have been used to living. Yet, with 'pandemic' a more insidious exception is at play which we can explore critically by delving into the semantics of pandemic. We start with the book. In the Oxford English Dictionary, 'pandemic' is designated as a term which can be used both as a noun and as an adjective. Philosophically speaking, that would mean that pandemic could be something in itself, like a substance or some concrete independent object; or a property of the former. As an adjective, pandemic means 'general, universal, widespread', or when it specifically relates to a disease, then it is an 'epidemic over a very large area; affecting a large proportion of a population. Also: of or relating to such a disease'. Finally, as an adjective, it can mean 'of or relating to physical or sensual love (as opposed to spiritual or divine love)'. As a noun, it is 'a pandemic disease; an outbreak of such a disease'.[12]

Even with these preliminary definitions by the book we can trace the workings of the state of exception. What is excepted here is the demos, the people from which the term gets its full reference and meaning. First, something widespread is not necessarily universal or general. The latter refers to a totality, to the meaning of the 'pan'. 'Pan' refers to a totality like in a panopticon. With the term 'panopticon' we mean a structure from which one can see and/or be seen from *all* sides. Using a term with 'pan' without referring to a totality is at least inaccurate. At the same time, in 'pandemic', the 'all' refers or is inextricably linked to demos, that is, to the people of a polis; its citizens. However, in these preliminary definitions the conceptual core of 'demos', and, concomitantly, its political meaning, is excluded. To be precise, it is excluded in its inclusion since a disease applies to all living things, and as such to human beings as living beings. In the exceptional medical meaning of 'pandemic', the demos is stripped of its political dimension and it refers simply to bare life where a disease can be obtained.

Moreover, in ancient times 'demos' could refer either to all people in all city states in general or just the citizens of a single city state. Technically, something occurring only in Athens, as a city state, as a demos, could be referred to as pandemic. Athens could thus be in a pandemic state whereas Sparta or any other city state would not. Demos is already a totality, that is, all the citizens of a polis *with no exception*. Adding the totality of 'pan' in the political concept of 'demos' does not constitute a literary pleonasm. Rather, with these two totalities the aim was to refer to all political possibilities with no exception. 'Pandemic' is not only about the summation of individuals, but the totality of the polis, of all praxis as political. Just as Being, as Heidegger (1962) keeps repeating in *Being and Time*, is not the summation of beings, equally, a polis is not just the summation of its individuals or the things that make it up individually. A gathering of all citizens of a polis *with no exception* is one of the inceptual realisations of the term 'pandemic'.[13] Such 'pandemic' means that all the functions of the polis come to a halt as everyone gathers up for a common purpose. Such suspension of the polis in its entirety constitutes an authentic pandemic. It is not that a pandemic causes a suspension, but the suspension is (a) pandemic. The common (political) purpose which could entail a pandemic is crucial since in its absence we would have a *pandem*onium rather than a *pandem*ic.

The passing which leads to the point where 'pandemic' refers only to a disease is a symptom, in the full sense of the term, a symptom of the diseased, the asthenic thinking of bare life. The disease here is a de-ceased 'demos'; the ceasing of the political reference of demos. To understand this further, we will have to delve into the semantic logic of biological thinking.

As we saw in the definitions of the book, a pandemic, in the biological sense as a widespread disease, is being defined through something that it is not, that is, an epidemic. According to the dictionary of epidemiology, epidemic is '[from the Greek epi (upon), demos (people)] The occurrence in a community or region of cases of an illness, specific health-related behavior, or other health-related events clearly in excess of normal expectancy' (p. 60). Similarly, a pandemic is 'an epidemic occurring worldwide or over a very wide area, crossing international boundaries and usually affecting a large number of people' (p. 131). There is clearly an excess of normal expectancy in these definitions but an excess of a different kind than of health-related events. This excess is, first of all, semantic and has its source not in the outbreak of a virus as a disease, but in the thinking that constitutes 'pandemic' as a disease.

Reading closely the definitions above, when an epidemic occurs worldwide it becomes a pandemic – or it evolves into a pandemic. In other words, a pandemic cannot be if it does not first pass from the stage of an epidemic. *Simpliciter*, only an epidemic can *evolve* into a pandemic. What we see in these definitions is that 'epidemic' and 'pandemic' are now semantically related through a health-related code, what we normally call biological, when initially they were ideally related through the terminological and conceptual core of 'demos'. In the biological code, where the ideal or cultural part of these terms has been consumed by bare life, two initially distinct phenomena, epidemic and pandemic, end up being related through the code of evolution. Yet, this evolution is of a virus, of a disease. The only difference between 'epidemic' and 'pandemic' in the biological code which excepts the political meaning of demos is a matter of quantification of the spread of a disease, of bodies affected.[14] Demos is (pan-demically) deceased by being (semantically) dis-eased.

As we saw earlier, 'demos' refers to a totality. A disease which affects all the citizens of a polis would be an epidemic *not a pandemic*. Precisely because 'demos' is a concept referring to a totality of citizens, an epidemic in its non-exceptional meaning would refer to all citizens. When Agamben (2021) refers to the phenomenon coded COVID-19, he justly uses only the term epidemic since, indeed, the virus affects the demos.[15] Something epidemic does not need to lead to the dissolution of the polis or the suspension of the political as it happened in the ancient times in the cases of 'pandemic' or 'pandemonium'. A pandemic, however, would immediately entail the polis being, like Hobbes describes in the *Leviathan*, *tanquuam dissoluta*, as if dissolved, precisely because a pandemic, like a general gathering, puts the polis in suspension. In Homer, Agamben rightly observes, civil war is described as an epidemic. Civil war takes place within the polis not outside it. The sides of the war make up its demos. Civil war is an epidemic since not all functions of the polis are suspended, yet it affects the demos as a totality of citizens.

The transvaluation of the terms 'pandemic' and 'epidemic' as types of diseases mirrors the state of exception in the political domain that Agamben has described. To make this clearer, we need to focus on the constitution of 'pandemic'. In the terms 'epidemic' and 'pandemic', as in all words, the letters, as elements that signify, constitute the physical/material aspect of the name, and the meaning of the name is its ideal part, its meaning, its signification. In the biological appropriation of the terms, the meaning of 'demos' is excepted; only the material/physical aspect of it, the 'demos' as a collection of letters and sounds, mere bodies, is what remains and allows for the two terms to be related biologically – while excluding the ideal meaning of 'demos' as the totality of the citizens of a state. For an epidemic to be related to a pandemic through the biological code, where the latter is an evolution of the former, the letters, as simple material bodies, have consumed, exhausted, included in their exclusion, the ideal meaning through which they originally came to be. This transvaluation also mirrors the phenomenon of the exception becoming the rule. The biological sense of the term 'pandemic' was an exception whereas now it has discursively become the rule consuming its authentic sense.

With this semantic exploration we can see that language does indeed reflect or mirror the world in another sense than the platonic one. What we have as a mirror image is the exception that is taking place in the juridico-political order. Whereas Agamben, following Foucault, seems to avoid ascribing responsibility for the allowance of such exception, in this chapter, we take the Sartrean side and resist the depersonalisation, another form of exception, which takes place when we reify our praxes. The taking place of the nihilistic state of exception amounts to a responsibility which befalls on every living being as critical or every critical being who suspends its critical possibility.

BEING CRITICAL OR CALLING FOR A NECESSITY TO EXCEPT THE BIOLOGICAL PANDEMIC

When we characterise something as 'pandemic' we do not just undertake a simple labelling. To characterise something as such means to undertake a judgement. And the judgement carries with it an existential stipulation (see Husserl, 1973). So, when we say that we are currently in a pandemic, then the following things are happening. First, we have judged that there is such a thing as a pandemic – and, at best, we know what it is. Second, there is something specific that is taking place now. Finally, that which is taking place now is a pandemic – as in matching what we know to be a pandemic as such with what is currently taking place. This may seem trivial, yet the philosophical implications are vast.[16] Now, even if someone or a group decides to label something as 'pandemic', in other words to baptise it, then, if we use the same term to refer it, then that means that we accept, implicitly or explicitly, both the constitution of that something as something and its baptism. That is, by coming to terms with it, by allowing that same discourse, then we are equally responsible as the baptisers even if we did not term it as such.[17]

Naming something carries with it a normative element which creates certain expectations. Philosophically, naming something 'table' comes with certain affordances. By bringing a table to mind one conceives immediately that that which is named 'table' cannot be used as a brush for instance – by definition.[18] Each name is, among other things, a guideline for thinking. In a recent scientific study by Singer et al. (2021), this point is verified by showing quantitatively that depending on what kind of definition one chooses to accept for a biological pandemic, then the assessment of its risk will also vary; and, deductively, the measures mandated to be taken to tackle it will also vary within the biological code. The definition of what constitutes a pandemic created a mass controversy in 2011 with the outbreak of H1N1 virus to the point that the WHO had to change its definition in order to provide a justification for the measures to be taken to tackle it. [19] This shows, once again, that before the biological comes the political – and in the political there lies judgement as decision. At the same time, we can observe here that once it is picked up by the biological code, 'pandemic' is being emptied of its primary signification through the multiplication of its definitions. Just like a product loses, through its excessive reproduction, its original use, and exchange value as related to the labour that allowed it to be, so 'pandemic' loses the 'demos' in the excessive and exceptional biological (re)definitions.

Being critical means suspending the naïve ontology by asking radical questions. Has the disease affected everyone as an individual? The answer is patently obviously 'no.' Let us now think 'pandemic' in the biological code. On which definition shall we work? The one in the dictionary of epidemiology or the one on which the WHO has decided to work after its many revisions? We notice that these revisions are not based on any scientific data. With whatever definition one decides to work, then one thing is evident: a double exception. Let us see how.

In all biological appropriations of 'pandemic' the individual is lost and becomes a state or some sort of geographical topology. The individual is excepted since the virus cannot affect something ideal like the boundaries of a state or a geography, but the people who might be inhabiting them. Even if we take each country or state as a citizen of the world and, thus, we change the reference from people to states – which would mean exemplifying the individual through the whole, that is, excepting the individuality of the individual – still, the use of the term 'pandemic' is incorrect, since there are plenty of countries or states in the globe which have not been affected by the virus.[20] Even thinking through the biological code, we experienced an epidemic not a pandemic.

In whatever code, when we use 'pandemic' or 'epidemic' without the intention of referring to the totality of the people that these terms imply, we are thinking metonymically. Metonymy is grounded on exception and can be dangerous. As Agamben underscores in most of his works, metonymy implies a desemanticisation and suspension of reference to the real. In our COVID-19 times, when we give in to the discursive use of 'pandemic' we allow the application of a floating exceptional signifier which takes over the real without really applying to it. Just like in the state of exception, the juridical law is suspended while its norm is in force without being applied, so too, our discursive use of 'pandemic' suspends *our judgement* while its norm, during the discursive use of the term, applies a judgmental force without a judgement authentically having taken place. When we use the term 'pandemic' to refer to the phenomenon coded COVID-19 we decide to not judge or we judge in an asthenic way.

Thinking logically, rather than metonymically, the term 'pandemic' cannot have a correct reference to the real even if we work within the biological code and its many versions. As we allow the discursive use of 'pandemic', we perpetuate a false reference – or a reference which is based on the logic of exception. By using the term 'pandemic' in its exceptional biological signification we make use of an exceptional signifier. By excepting the demos from whom its meaning is primarily derived, it becomes a virtual signifier referring to something simulated rather than real. When the pandemic is biologically appropriated its reference undergoes a 'death sentence' as Baudrillard often says for every such simulacrum. It is not that it loses its representational power, but, instead, this power is exhausted in displacing the main reference from which it derives its meaning: the totality of human existence. Biological pandemic, impossible to refer to it, is essentially a hyperreal pandemic.

THE HYPERREALITY OF THE PANDEMIC

The term 'hyperreality' belongs to Baudrillard. The relevance of the thought of Baudrillard with respect to the current situation, especially in regard to the virtualisation of everything, has already started to being explored (see Ehsen & Allam, 2021). What has not been explored yet is how the passing to virtualisation, or what Baudrillard calls the hyperreal, requires the structure of a state of exception as a condition for its happening. One way to understand hyperreality and its relation to the pandemic that never took place is through the phenomenon of simulation. In *Simulations*, Baudrillard (1983) writes:

> To dissimulate is to feign not to have what one has. To simulate is to feign to have what one hasn't. One implies a presence, the other an absence. But the matter is more complicated, since to simulate is not simply to feign: 'Someone who feigns an illness can simply go to bed and make believe he is ill. Some who simulates an illness produces in himself some of the symptoms'. (Littre) (p. 5)

Feigning to have what one has not or the production of what is related to what is simulated is, as we said earlier, an *as if* structure. The one who simulates an illness has all the symptoms *as if* they were ill. But if to define the occurrence of an illness, or to identify its existence, the relation to the symptoms is absolutely required, then there is no way to tell the difference between the two. This 'as if' is as real as if an actual illness would have taken place. The possibility of distinguishing a real illness from a simulated one would be impossible. Another example:

> Go and organise a fake hold-up .... Demand ransom, and arrange it so that the operation creates the greatest commotion possible-in brief, stay close to the 'truth', so as to test the reaction of the apparatus to a perfect simulation. But you won't succeed the web of artificial signs will be inextricably mixed up with real elements (a police officer will really shoot on sight; a bank customer will faint and die of a heart attack; they will really turn the phoney ransom mer to you) – in brief, you will unwittingly find yourself immediately in the real, one of whose functions is precisely to devour every attempt at simulation, to reduce everything to some reality – that's exactly how the established order is, well before institutions and justice come into play. (p. 43)

In a simulation, we are found *immediately in the real* and because this real is more than real, it is hyperreal.[21]

In the book *The Gulf War Never Took Place*, which includes Baudrillard's (1991) three interventions, we learn that the hyperreal as a simulacrum, as something with no referent, or, even better, as something with a hollow reference, with an empty reference, cannot take place without some sort of a nihilist act. The latter, in the case of the Gulf War, is structurally analogous with what Agamben calls the state of exception. What was excepted, both in the Gulf War and the war against COVID-19, has been the political deliberation as one would expect in a parliamentary democracy. Politics pass to 'the absence of politics pursued by other means' (p. 30). And the other means here involves 'promotion and speculation' (p. 30).

From the start, the upsurge of media communication about a deadly virus was carried out with no, if any, real evidence. The first lockdown was an act carried out with no evidence of its efficacy. The absence of images of supposed full hospitals with patients was covered, in all senses of coverage, with endless talks and reports about deaths – just like in the Gulf War. But even the quantification of the latter has been more or less speculative. Apart from the fact that no biopsies were done to warrant that the cause of death was indeed the virus in a causal efficacy, in the beginning, up until the tests were put into circulation, all reporting of cases and deaths were purely speculative – just like in the Gulf War (Baudrillard, 1991, p. 73).[22]

Even to the day, the registration of COVID-19 deaths is done speculatively. Insofar as someone has passed or has been diagnosed with COVID-19 prior to their passing away they would be registered as dying out of COVID-19. The very idea of the scientific Pearson correlation is purely excepted. Yet, the excess of reporting and promoting the idea of a deadly virus which will affect everyone has been relentless. This excess is similar to the excess of information that was covering the Gulf War as Baudrillard (1991) reported – in brackets the analogy with the pandemic:

> Unlike earlier wars [virus outbreaks] in which there were political aims either of conquest [raising awareness] or domination [educating the public in how to be protected], what is at stake in this one is the war [outbreak] itself: its status, its meaning, its future. It is beholden not to have an objective but to prove its very existence. (p. 32)

Everything was taking place *as if* there was a pandemic.

Let us work through the classical phenomenological register. In classical phenomenological terms, nothing or very little was itself given *in intuition*, immediately, in *propria persona* as Husserl would say, that could allow a meaning fulfilment of a pandemic – even if we relied strictly on its biological sense. Instead, what was given was a relentless mediated explosion of information, or, to use another of Baudrillard's terms, a pornography of information, supplementing what should have been given in order for our concept of pandemic to be empirically fulfilled adequately or in apodeictic certainty. No matter the definition of pandemic one wishes to accept, if a phenomenological reduction is properly undertaken, then no phenomenologist could ever justify apodeictic certainty from the given that a pandemic has been taking place. All that was given in intuition was (mass-)mediated *not immediate*. What was given to intuition was images and representations from the media *as if* there were a pandemic. In other words, the given were signs which were aiming to convince just like a television advertisement.

No pandemic was experienced phenomenologically speaking. A pandemic was consumed. As Baudrillard (1996) explains in *The System of Objects*, consumption is not absorption or assimilation. 'Consumption is *the virtual totality of all objects and messages presently constituted in a more less coherent discourse*. Consumption, in so far as it is meaningful, is *a systematic act of the manipulation of signs*' (p. 210). The virus as a sign was encoded in a more or less coherent discourse to be consumed as a pandemic.

> We can see that what is consumed are not objects but the relation itself – signified and absent, included and excluded at the same time – it is, *the idea of the relation* that is consumed in the series of objects which manifests it. (p. 210)

A pandemic was consumed, it was never experienced, it never took place.

Moreover, just like the Gulf War, this outbreak is an outbreak of excesses. In his interventions, Nancy (in Castrillon & Marchechsky, 2021) was trying to point out that the exception in which the outbreak consists is viral in all senses – 'an entire civilization is in question, there is no doubt about it. There is a sort of viral exception – biological, computer-scientific, cultural – which is pandemic' (p. 27). Imported from abroad, like other products and put into circulation, the 'coronavirus pandemic, is on every level, a product of globalization' (p. 63). And this globalisation with its virality, is an effect of capitalism which has, like a virus, affected the whole globe. If anything, it is not the virus which has created a pandemic but capitalism as (a) pandemic which works like a viral disease and affects everyone. Capitalism is, in a sense, pandemic, COVID-19 is not.

Capitalism and excess go together. In a time when European countries were deploring financial crises, cutting down wages, and raising taxes, we witnessed a full deployment of excessive commercial campaigns in the effort of masking a pandemic which was not, at least, yet there. The commodification of masks, the luxury packaging of the lateral flow tests, the advertising campaigns, and the spokespersons promoting isolation and then vaccination; the variety of vaccines offered to the consumer as a choice, yet a mandatory choice; all this, among so many other things, make this pandemic a pure spectacle of excess – 'a [pandemic] between excessive, superabundant and overequipped societies ... committed both to waste (including human waste) and the necessity of getting rid of it' (Baudrillard, 1991, p. 33). The waste here is both the virus in its potential to waste lives and also human lives; humans who passed away and who were treated like waste and not given the chance of proper burial.[23] Once again, in such excess a nihilating act of exception applies to the symbolic meaning of coming to terms with death – in this case, the death of the Other.

Just like in the Gulf War, the biological 'pandemic' followed the logic of distance. The social distancing that was mandated as a measure in dealing with the virus is analogous to the distancing in the Gulf War. The latter happened from a distance. As Baudrillard explains, nothing happened on the battlefield. What took place was from a distance *as if* the whole globe became a battlefield. The distance here plays exactly the same role of deterrence as in the COVID-19 'pandemic': to prevent the event of actually taking place while promoting that it is already taking place. As we saw earlier, the initial meaning of pandemic requires bodies coming together united in a purpose whereas here the distancing is excepting the proximity required for a pandemic in order to deter it. This seems like a paradox, yet this is precisely how the logic of deterrence operates (see Tunander, 1989). The logic of deterrence is the logic of exception in the pretext of security. Deterrence is not prevention. To deter one has to exclude what one has already included exhaustively in order to secure themselves from it, like in the case of terrorism: '... what kind of state would be capable of dissuading and annihilating all terrorism in the bud ...? It would have to arm itself with such terrorism and generalize terror on every level ... this is the price of security ...' (Baudrillard, 2002, p. 32).

The Gulf War was an act in the logic of deterrence and so was the virus COVID-19 coded 'pandemic'. The war metaphor was prevalent in describing the supposed pandemic attack of the virus. The phenomenon coded COVID-19 was constituted as an invisible enemy attacking us and from which we would have to defend ourselves at all costs. In the Gulf War, we followed Baudrillard, there was no battlefield. The whole globe became a battlefield and the same thing happened with COVID-19, pace the states which were not affected, the states that excepted themselves from the exception. In the war against COVID-19 everyone individually was fighting against an invasive virus. The invasion of the virus, however, was as invisible as the virus itself, as was the fighting. Agamben (2021) wrote that a 'war that can occupy any one of us is the most absurd of wars .... The enemy is not outside, but within' (p. 6). Strictly speaking, the enemy was everywhere neither inside nor outside. The absurdity of the war was reflected in the absurdity of the measures *as if* staying behind closed doors would barricade us against the invisible invasive enemy – see Godfrey-Smith (2021) for a further elaboration of the absurdity of the measures. Becoming invisible socially *as if* barricading from an invisible invasive virus is a logic of deterrence not of prevention.

But let us dwell a bit on the war metaphor. As Panzeri (2021) has insightfully noticed,

> The use of war metaphors is a widespread strategy in public speech for framing and representing the challenges to be faced. US Presidents declared war against poverty (Johnson, 1964), crime (Johnson, 1965), drugs (Nixon, 1971), cancer (Nixon, 1971), inflation (Ford, 1977); but this metaphor is so ubiquitous that it can also involve apparently not belligerent enemies such as traffic jams, sunshine and even salad. (Panzeri, 2021, p. 9)

However, the use of the military metaphor is not just a rhetorical device employed by the media. In fact, as Babich (2015) showed, the whole western 'scientific' medicine is based on this metaphor as if a disease happens when an offensive virus attacks an organism deemed a closed unit. We remain 'persuaded by this invasive schematism, so much so, that the notion instantiates the persistence of the standard view or normal idea of disease causality, even the contrary evidence is taken proof of precisely what is pre-supposed' (p. 21).

The use of the war metaphor enables to ground the necessity of necessity in order to pass to the state of exception – after all, it is in the name of security against an invasive enemy that the suspension of the political has always been justified as Agamben has shown. It is for protecting the demos from a war that a state of exception could be justifiably decided by the sovereign. In the case of COVID-19, however, we did not have a sovereign in the classical sense who decided the necessity and called for exception. The decision which marks the borders between authority and sovereignty was lost somewhere among the institutions be they political, medical, or mass media. There was no decision in the classical sense and that is why it is now difficult to ascribe responsibility for calling an exception. That does not mean that sovereignty is lost. Sovereignty is now 'not the result of a specific decision but of the social and legal order' (Silva & Higuera, 2021). Baudrillard's (1996) concept of the code is apt here.[24] It is the medical code which grounded the necessity of necessity. It would be futile to say that this or that president or prime minister decided. Decision requires judgement and the latter is consumed in the medical code.

Let us pull those threads together: deterrence, war, and exception. The distancing that has been promoted in the name of viral deterrence results in maximising uncertainty and fear to the point of terror. Unable to objectify the fear leads to permanent anxiety and indeterminacy both of which widen the space for the media to shape the real (Agamben, 2021, p. 49). Concomitantly, this results in perpetuating the virtual reality for the distanced spectators, who end up being 'a rarefied mass founded on prohibition, but for that very reason, especially passive and compact' (p. 15). The logic of deterrence in this instance works in terms of excepting the possibility of coming to terms with what actually happened. While being afraid, unable to come together and deliberate and rationalise the threat, purely deterred, paralysed, and excepted, even stupefied as both Baudrillard and Agamben characterise them, the spectators are unable to think and accept what is offered to them like the spectators in Plato's cave.

We could use the metaphor of enslavement and say that in the logic deterrence, the logic of hyperreal prevention, we were enslaved. This enslavement, however, was virtual. The question, now, is the following: Why do we not resist or react to this enslavement? Why do we play along without being critical about it?

HYPERREAL DETERRENCE OF PANDEMIC

The biological appropriation of 'pandemic' excepts the demos. By such an exception it equally excludes conceiving its possibilities. The ultimate possibility of 'demos' pandemically is death. The normalisation of biological discourse in terms of conceiving causes of death excepts the event of death which is always already taking place pandemically. Death as an event which is happening now pandemically can only be accelerated or decelerated; it cannot be caused. The very idea of cause is a form of exception of the real. Our concern is with causes of death *as if* death can be caused. Heidegger tried to explain this with the expression 'leveling down'.

For Heidegger, our concerns are always already defined and interpreted by what he calls the *They*:

> We take pleasure and enjoy ourselves as *they* take pleasure; we read, see, and judge about literature and art as *they* see and judge; ... we find 'shocking' what *they* find shocking. The 'they' which is nothing definite and which all are, though not as the sum, prescribes the kind of Being of everydayness. (p. 164)[25]

One way to interpret Heidegger's *They* is to think about the cultural framework in which one is born into until the time they can realise themselves as they are, until they can have their own self-awareness. The *they*, alternatively, is/are the one(s) who is/are able to define what is and impose it as real, as common sense, as everydayness.

We are born and raised within a particular perception and appreciation of how the world is. This perception and appreciation, if there is any difference between the two, comes from this *They* which also directs to a distinctive set of possibilities for us. Although this *They* is not an actual embodied subject, it still is 'the Realest subject' of everydayness which dictates, in one way or another, the how of our lives. Very often Heidegger describes the *They* with that common sense which underlies our everyday discourse. To bring this closer to Baudrillard, the *They constitutes our code of* ... ; be it communication, behaviour, thinking, and so on. As something in which we are found ourselves without actively having contributed to its shaping; something in which we are consumed in, this common sense or code is for Heidegger an inauthentic way of being. We are inauthentic when we lose ourselves in the ways *they* think and act. This inauthenticity is a form of idleness or an asthenia since we are lost, or better, carried away in/by the ways *they* think and act. As we commerce with the world as 'the they-self' (p. 167), the *they* distorts a very important aspect of our being there, our Dasein, as Heidegger calls it. *They* distort our being towards death into a being of death. *They* interpret death as something 'bad' which is or should not be part of our being when in fact it is an essential part of our Dasein. The discourse, the talk about death by the *They* is done in a 'fugitive manner' (Heidegger, 1962, p. 297) as an occurrence in the world which is happening somewhere, to someone but 'not right now'. *They* act *as if* death does not affect us *as if* it has nothing to do with us now. The now for us is the everydayness of the world in our actual and possible concerns. For the *They* the now is life, and death, its 'opposite', should not concern us.

If logos is to be interpreted as reason, then such an interpretation of death goes beyond it. Such logos comes as an unprecedented para-logy, since death is distorted. In this distortion death is supposed to be caused and it is not thought to be taking place now. It is *as if* it will occur somewhere, somehow, whereas in reality it takes place anytime, anywhere, anyway, right now. Our being which is a being towards death is an event which, for Heidegger, is happening presently, it takes place now, rather than, as *they* think, being something that could happen at one point in time. Living is at the same time and place dying, a being towards death while *they* conceal it. Insofar as we are born we are dying and this being towards death is concealed so that dying 'which is essentially mine in such a way that no-one can be my representative, is perverted into an event of public occurrence which the "they" encounters' (Heidegger, 1962, p. 297). We encounter death; we count it; idly as in 'there were five dead in that accident', but not recount it; we are encountering it by *dis*counting death while giving prominence to numbers – 's/he was 80 years old'. *They* consume it through numbers. With such consumption, the dead and death are held at bay. This is precisely how death as the only pandemic is being excepted with COVID-19. In the case of COVID-19, death as a pandemic reality is converted into a fear of death through a disease which is supposedly pandemic. Death is not faced, but quantified, counte(re)d not encounte(re)d. Thus, by excepting the individual person, by excluding their subjectivity and including them only as diseased bodies, the dead are kept at bay as if they are part of a disease which is pandemic.

This way of economising death is for Heidegger a fugitive way of dealing with it. It is a way of understanding it which treats it as something with which we should not interfere; *as if* it should not be our concern. This deviant way of living our being aims at transforming the anxiety that our being unto death brings into a fear of something with the prospect of overcoming it. Our being unto death is for Heidegger our ultimate possibility and *they* try to make us overcome it either by forgetting about it or by thinking that it is usually caused by something and thus to be dealt with biologically. Peter Singer (1980) writes:

> If I think that [death] is likely to happen at any moment, my present existence will be fraught with anxiety, and will presumably [?] be less enjoyable than if I do not think it is likely to happen for some time. *If I learn that people like myself are very rarely killed*, I will worry less. (p. 91, emphasis added)

This attitude of acting *as if* death is not *likely to happen* to me/us *for some time*, this pretension or, one could easily say hypocrisy, allows us to numb the anxiety of our ultimate potentiality of being and make life more enjoyable, *presumably*. *I will worry less* since I will (p)resume that *people like myself are very rarely killed*. By showing such an attitude I am attuned with the *they* and feel strong and healthy as I am able to overcome this fear of death which 'gets passed off as a weakness with which no self-assured Dasein may have any acquaintance' (Heidegger, 1962, p. 298). A healthy, living Dasein is self-assured, and *will worry less, presumably*. In this way, Dasein is alienated from its authentic Being which is manifested when one's ownmost potentiality for Being, being towards death, is concealed or suppressed in one's own daily circumspective concern. In the workings of the *They* '*One* never dies, and a certain form of im-mortality might even represent one of the ultimate constituent features of the "They"' (Courtine, 1991, p. 80). *They* force Dasein towards a 'mode of an untroubled indifference *towards* the uttermost possibility of existence' (Heidegger, 1962, p. 299).

This 'acting *as if*' is a modality which directs us to realise and potentialise ourselves without appreciating our a priori ownmost potentiality for Being which is Death. Our possibilities receive their horizon by what *they* determine, interpret, and restrict about our being unto death. Our being unto death is thus levelled down and our being becomes idle, asthenic, and inauthentic. This inauthentic way of dealing with our being bars all the potentialities of who we are which would accrue if our being unto death was genuinely appreciated. Who we are can only be revealed authentically when we resolve this alienation which *they* perpetuate. We are authentic when we resolve while anticipating our being unto death which Heidegger refers to in many places as anticipatory resolution. This movement resolves first of all the ties with the *they* which masks our being by levelling down and restricting our being unto death. Unless this resolution takes place we would constantly be consumed in the *they* while at the same time perpetuate its idle talk just like in the case of what *they* constituted as COVID-19. Unless this resolution takes place, we would judge as *they* do(es). COVID-19 comes as a brilliant example of what Heidegger has explained as *they* and the levelling down of our being that *they* do(es).

They (have) constitute(d) COVID-19 as (a) pandemic. Death is constituted as a result of this virus which is to be overcome through a lockdown, a medical treatment, and so on. While COVID-19 could have been an opportunity for an authentic anticipation of death, of an authentic isolation, it has ended up being objectified through fear as if it could be overcome. In the case of the way the COVID-19 was handled, the present was suppressed, suspended, and forced to be locked into the ennui of lockdowns. There could have been an opportunity for an authentic resolution but this did not take place precisely because the real pandemic was excepted into a biological pandemic and thus dealt with in a fugitive manner. But this exception refers to the only possible pandemic that could be: the reality of the totality of the human condition: death.

As Agamben (2021) underscored, with Christianity, the anxiety of death was deferred with the promise of an afterlife. With the present biological nihilism, the anxiety of death is excepted, since there are no possibilities left for the individual to explore in terms of dealing with it as the only real pandemic – since the latter is now defined as caused by a disease or something for which the religion of medicine can provide an antidote, a vaccine. Precisely because today the new religion of science and medicine has 'become mandatory and legally enforceable' (p. 28), the individual is left without being able to make an authentic resolution for their ultimate potentiality. At the same time, by supplementing death as pandemic with a disease as pandemic, the anxiety of authentic pandemic is reversed into a perpetual fear with no object, with no reference; hyperreal:

> If we look at the state of exception which we are now experiencing we could say that the medical religion combines the perpetual crisis of capitalism with a Christian idea of the end of times of an eschaton where the extreme decision is constantly ongoing and where the end is simultaneously crushed and deferred in any incessant effort to govern it. (p. 38)

Yet, a last question remains to be asked: why do we not resolve the *they*, which as the medical code today, is consumed without being put into crisis?

Even if we accept Agamben's analysis that capitalism has been mixed with Christianity and biology in simulating the possibility of overcoming death, we still miss an exegesis of how this unfolds. We are also still thinking in a state of exception since our thinking excepts the individuals – Christianity, capitalism, and biology. A working hypothesis is that we are seduced by this code. Baudrillard (2001) has paid attention to the workings of seduction. 'Seduction is that which extracts meaning from discourse and detracts it from its truth' (p. 53). The discourse is the medical code. Truth, which, if it is truth, is necessarily pandemic, is death. We are seduced by the medical code *as if* in it we could overcome death. 'Seduction is itself vertiginous, being the effect not of simple attraction, but of an attraction that is redoubled in a sort of challenge to or fatality of its essence' (Baudrillard, 1990, p. 27). Seduction is a hyperreal attraction, too much attraction or attraction coming from both sides.

The medical code seduces like an advertisement. It is not coincidental that the limitations in the case of COVID-19 were being advertised just like a product to be consumed. In advertising, there is seduction because there is 'the spinning of use-value and exchange-value into annihilation in the pure and empty form of the brand-name' (Baudrillard, 1990, p. 187). It is not, however, the advertising or what is signified in it that is seductive. In being seduced, the responsibility does not lie in the discourse even if we say that something is seductive. A seductive discourse is the one with which we do not engage; the one with which we do not enter a relationship of exchange. In being seduced, there is a certain inertia which is a result of actively being passive, we let it take us away.

An example of such active passivity was revealed in the slogan the UK employed to seduce us for abiding by the restrictions: 'Save the NHS, to save lives'. This slogan is first of all ambiguous. If we think it through as a speech act then we can ask: To what does it aspire? The illocutionary form, what is intending to do, is ambiguous. Is it an imperative, a wish, a promise? This indeterminacy pushes the responsibility of saving to the individual. I say to you what I need you to do in order to save everyone. And what I need you to do is nothing – isolate, be actively passive. But most importantly, your right to health is a provision by the NHS, that is, instead of the NHS saving you, you need, you are now obligated to save the NHS to save you. We saw it earlier and we see it now. The right to health is turned dialectically into an obligation. The overtones of what Nietzsche called Christian slave morality are overflowing. Yet, the thread of relevance here is the active passivity, the inertia of seduction of being a saviour by doing nothing.

We are *seduced* by the medico-capitalistico-Christian code. We are actively passive and do not engage with it critically. It is our

> secret form of the refusal of the will, of an in-voluntary challenge to everything which was demanded of the subject of philosophy – that is to say, to all rationality of choice and to all exercise of will, of knowledge and of liberty. (Baudrillard & Maclean, 1985, p. 585)

Philosophy starts when death is realised – in all senses of the word, even in the platonic, $\mu\varepsilon\lambda\acute{\varepsilon}\tau\alpha\iota\ \theta\alpha\nu\acute{\alpha}\tau o\upsilon$. We are seduced and that is why we are not being critical or why we suspend our critical being. We actively allow our being to keep taking place in a state of exception.

Seduction always rests on an uncertainty of desire (Baudrillard, 1990). This uncertainty is for life and equally for death: we do not know why we live for and thus we do not know why we die for.[26] The seduction into the discourse of COVID-19 coded pandemic allows for normalising the exception of realising the event of the authentic pandemic, death. It is a fatal strategy. Just like in Baudrillard's example of taking hostage which never took place as reality but as hyperreality, so with COVID-19, a pandemic never took place in reality but in the hyperreality of seduction.

NOTES

1. The chapter was written during the last phase of the so-called pandemic, hence the references to the 'present' and the 'past two' years.

2. Agamben has made various interventions throughout this year and in many different outlets. For convenience, all references can be traced to the recent bound edition which includes all of them: Giorgio Agamben (2021), *Where Are We Now? The Epidemic as Politics*.

3. In this part, we are just adumbrating crudely the key concepts which are required for our critical exploration. By no means do we intend here to delve into the nuances of Schmitt's political analyses. One should read Agamben's (2005) *State of Exception* for a detailed analysis of Schmitt's animadversions.

4. In the *State of Exception*, Agamben (2005) will clarify genealogically how this inscription has evolved over time in the various political institutions in the West. A point to note is that the beginning of this inscription is traced to the Roman Law and not before. In the ancient democratic system, the possibility of suspending the law, in whatever form it existed, rested on the demos not the law which was a product of the former.

5. This is a crucial point and needs to be understood in its entirety. For example, in our mainstream thinking about how anything, how the world, comes to be, we usually have two main options that form a dialectic: creation or evolution, being or becoming. Nietzsche overcame this dialectic by following Heraclitus and positing that the world is *now happening*. If the world had been created, it would have already been finished, there would have been no world anymore – see Deleuze (1983, pp. 40–45) and our discussion of Heraclitus (Ioannidis, 2021a).

6. Exemplification requires exception. cf. Agamben's (1998) *Homo Sacer* for a complete analysis of the structure of exemplification and Heidegger's and Fink's analysis of Heraclitus (Heidegger and Fink, 1979).

7. The analogy with the 'witness' requires special mention since it is a key analogy used to describe the human condition both in Agamben and in Derrida. See Agamben's (1999) *Remnants of Auschwitz: The Witness and the Archive* and Blanchot and Derrida's (2000) *The Instant of My Death*.

8. Just for being philosophically accurate, thinking for Heidegger takes place only when human existence comes to terms with being there, in this threshold, this schism in which human existence is found. Agamben's (2000) thinking is analogous (see *Theory Out of Bounds*).

9. For Heidegger's approach to thinking, see also Babich (2016).

10. A host of scientists raised concerns about the panic of this outbreak in the beginning. Concerns about the scientific evidence provided were constantly raised (see Abbasi, 2020 and *The Guardian's* report of a poll of the fear of scientists to speak their expertise, https://www.theguardian.com/world/2021/oct/13/scientists-abused-and-threatened-for-discussing-COVID-global-survey-finds). Yet, if one attempts to explore these they would be accused of conspiracy – see Agamben's (2021) beautiful reply on this point.

11. See the very important analysis of Saidel (2014) in his comparison of Agamben's and Wittgenstein's use of the expression form(s) of life.

12. These definitions are available in https://www.oed.com/view/Entry/136746?redirectedFrom=pandemic#eid. The distinction between physical and divine or spiritual love as a sense for pandemic is attributed to Plato. A lot of genealogical work is required here to link this thread to bare life, but this goes beyond the scope of this chapter. Here, we are interested in showing how these very definitions rest on a thinking which reflects the political state of exception that Agamben identifies in the sociopolitical domain – the state of exception which has become the rule in politics is reflected analogously in language. As Wittgenstein (1958) noted, 'to imagine a language means to imagine a form of life' (p. 8); cf. Malcolm (1977).

13. See relevant entry in Liddell and Scott Dictionary online.

14. See also the discussion of Mitropoulos (2021) concerning that even these supposedly quantitative indices are essentially nationalist methods of classification.

15. In certain of his interviews, Agamben does use the term pandemic but these uses are a *lectio facilitor* and not philosophically significant.

16. For a more refined analysis of this process see Plato's *Cratylus*, Husserl (1973), and our discussion of the *Cratylus* in Ioannidis (2021a).

17. For the issue of baptism and discursivity see Apel (1994, 1998).

18. Peirce has painstakingly explained this process – see our analysis in Ioannidis (2019).

19. See the discussion between Barnett (2011), Doshi (2011), Kelly (2011), and Bonneux and Van Damme (2011).

20. According to the WHO and other sources, there are plenty of countries that have not reported any of their citizens affected by this virus. See https://www.usnews.com/news/best-countries/slideshows/countries-without-reported-COVID-19-cases and https://COVID19.who.int/table. We are obviously leaving aside here the issue of what is quantified under the categories 'country' or 'geographical area' with respect to the water element in terms of creating a posology of how much ground has been covered by each virus. - cf. Richardson (2019).

21. See Weiss' (2011) careful analysis of how this process unfolds in reality through the structure of power and presence.

22. See also Godfrey-Smith's (2021) analysis concerning the impropriety of the measures with respect to their efficacy.

23. See the analyses of Nestor Braunstein in Castrillon and Marchevsky (2021) and our commentary in Ioannidis (2021b).

24. The code is a set of categories to which we subordinate our thinking and being. It is a system of significations with no living syntax but with a normative efficiency which directs thought and action. The Wachowskis understood the code as a matrix from which one cannot escape.

25. This is a schematic presentation of a more elaborate analysis of Heidegger's anticipatory resolution which could be found in Ioannidis (2021a).

26. See also Babich (2020).

ACKNOWLEDGEMENTS

I would like to thank Susan Stuart, Dennis Grammatikos, and Eleni Rizou for their helpful critical contributions while this chapter was being written. I would also like to thank the reviewers who provided me with amazing critical suggestions which helped me improve drastically the original version of this chapter. Finally, I would like to thank José María Rosales, Gonçalo Marcelo, and Hanna-Mari Kivistö who provided me with the opportunity to participate in the virtual workshop *Reconceptualizing the State of Exception and its Challenges to Democracy and Rights in Europe* which took place in June 2021 as a joint effort from the University of Jyväskylä and the University of Coimbra.

REFERENCES

Abbasi, K. (2020). COVID-19: Politicisation, "corruption," and suppression of science. *BMJ, 371*, m4425. https://doi.org/10.1136/bmj.m4425

Agamben, G. (1998). *Homo Sacer: Sovereign power and bare life* (D. Heller-Roazen, Trans.). Meridian.

Agamben, G. (1999). *Remnants of Auschwitz: The witness and the archive.* Zone Books.

Agamben, G. (2000). *Theory out of bounds* (V. Binetti & C. Casarino, Trans.). UMP.

Agamben, G. (2005). *State of exception* (K. Attell, Trans.). CUP.

Agamben, G. (2007). *Profanations* (J. Fort, Trans.). Zone Books.

Agamben, G. (2021). *Where are we now? The epidemic as politics* (V. Dani, Trans.). Eris.

Apel, K.-O. (1994). *Selected essays: Towards a transcendental semiotics* (E. Mendietta, Eds.). Humanities Press.

Apel, K.-O. (1998). *From a transcendental semiotic point of view* (M. Papastephanou, Ed.). MUP.

Babich, B. (2015). Calling science pseudoscience: Fleck's archaeologies of fact and Latour's 'Biography of an Investigation' in AIDS denialism and homeopathy. *International Studies in the Philosophy of Science, 29*, 1–39.

Babich, B. (2016). Heidegger's Jews: Inclusion/exclusion and Heidegger's antisemitism. *The Journal of the British Society of Phenomenology, 47*, 133–156.

Babich, B. (2020). *Philosophical reflections: Retrieving Agamben's questions.* https://babettebabich.uk/2020/04/30/retrieving-agambens-questions/

Barnett, D. J. (2011). Pandemic influenza and its definitional implications. *Bulletin World Health Organization, 89*, 539–540.

Baudrillard, J. (1983). *Simulations* (P. Foss, P. Patton, & P. Beitchman, Trans.). Semiotext(e).

Baudrillard, J. (1990). *Fatal strategies* (P. Beitchman & W. G. J. Niesluchowsk, Trans.). Semiotext(e).

Baudrillard, J. (1991). *The Gulf war did not take place*, trans. P. Patton. Bloomington, IN: UIP.

Baudrillard, J. (1996). *The system of objects* (J. Benedict, Trans.). Verso.

Baudrillard. J. (2001). *Seduction* (B. Singer, Trans.). CTHEORY BOOKS.

Baudrillard, J. (2002). *The spirit of terrorism* (C. Turner, Trans.). Verso.

Baudrillard, J., & Maclean, M. (1985). The masses: The implosion of the social in the media. *New Literary History, 16*, 577–589.

Blanchot, M., & Derrida, J. (2000). *The instant of my death: Fiction and testimony* (E. Rottenberg, Trans.). SUP.

Bonneux, L., & Van Damme, W. (2011). Health is more than influenza. *Bulletin World Health Organization, 89*, (7): 539–540.

Castrillon, F., & Marchevsky, T. (2021). *Coronavirus, psychoanalysis, and philosophy: Conversations on pandemics, politics, and society.* Routledge.

Coulter, G. (2005). Intersections and divergencies in contemporary theory: Baudrillard and Agamben on politics and the daunting questions of our time. *International Journal of Baudrillard Studies, 2*, 1–34.

Courtine, J.-F. (1991). Voice of conscience and call of being. In E. Cadava, P. Connor, & J.-L. Nancy (Eds.), *Who comes after the subject?* (pp. 79–93). Routledge.

Deleuze, G. (1983). *Nietzsche and philosophy* (H. Tomlinson, Trans.). CUP.
Derrida, J. (2008). *Psyche: Inventions of the other II* (P. Kamuf, Trans.). SUP.
Doshi, P. (2011). The elusive definition of pandemic influenza. *Bulletin of World Health Organization, 89*, 532–538.
Godfrey-Smith, P. (2021). COVID heterodoxy in three layers. *Monash Bioethics Review, 27*, 1–23. https://doi.org/10.1007/s40592-021-00140-6
Ehsen, Z. R., & Alam, K. (2021). COVID-19: An age of fear, simulacra, or reality? *Contemporary Social Science, 17*(2), 143–156. https://doi.org/10.1080/21582041.2021.1942964
Finlayson, J. G. (2010). "Bare life" and politics in Agamben's reading of Aristotle. *The Review of Politics, 72*, 97–126.
Harriman, B. (2019). *Melissus and eleatic monism*. CUP.
Heidegger, M. (1949). What is metaphysics? In *Existence and being* (R. F. C. Hull & A, Crick, Trans.). Henry Regnery Company.
Heidegger, M. (1962). *Being and time* (J. Macquarrie & E. Robinson, Trans.). Blackwell.
Heidegger, M. (1989). *Contributions to philosophy (from Enowning)* (P. Emad & K. Maly, Trans.). IUP.
Heidegger, M. (1998). *Pathmarks* (W. McNeill, Ed.), CUP.
Heidegger, M., & Fink, E. (1979). *Heraclitus seminar 1966/67* (C. H. Seibert, Trans.). UAP.
Heraclitus. (2010). *Apanta*. Trans. Tasos Falkos Arvanitakis. Zetros [Ηράκλειτος, (2010). Άπαντα, μτφ., Τάσος Φάλκος- Αρβανιτάκης. Αθήνα: Ζήτρος.].
Hume, D. (1896). *A treatise on human nature*. Clarendon Press.
Husserl, E. (1973). *Experience and judgment: Investigations in a genealogy of logic* (J. S. Churchill, Trans.). Routledge, Kegan & Paul.
Ioannidis, I. (2019). The other side of Peirce's Phaneroscopy. *Sophia Philosophical Review, 2*, 74–101.
Ioannidis, I. (2021a). *Altruism or the other as the essence of existence: A philosophical passage to being altruistic*. Brill.
Ioannidis, I. (2021b). Book review: Coronavirus, psychoanalysis, and philosophy: Conversations on pandemics, politics and society, edited by Fernando Castrillón and Thomas Marchevsky. *Teaching Philosophy, 44*(3), 385–389.
Kelly, H. (2011). The classical definition of a pandemic is not elusive. *Bulletin of World Health Organization, 89*, 540–541.
Malcolm, N. (1977). *Thought and knowledge*. CUP.
Mitropoulos, A. (2021). The pandemic and the pandemonium of European philosophy. *Political Geography, 84*, 102275. https://doi.org/10.1016/j.polgeo.2020.102275
Moote, L., & Moote, D. (2004). *The Great Plague*. JHUP.
Nietzsche, F. (1996). *Human all too human* (R. J. Hollingdale, Trans.). CUP.
Patton, C. (2011). Pandemic, empire and the permanent state of exception. *Economic and Political Weekly, 46*, 103–110.
Richardson, P. (2019). Sovereignty, the hyperreal, and taking back control. *Annals of the Association of Geographers, 109*, 1999–2015.
Saidel, M. L. (2014). Form(s)-of-life. Agamben's reading of Wittgenstein and the potential uses of a notion. *Trans/Form/Acao, Marilia, 37*, 163–186.
Schmitt, C. (1985). *Political theology* (G. Schwab & T. B. Strong, Trans.). MIT Press.
Schmitt, C. (2013). *Dictatorship* (M. Hoelzl & G. Ward, Trans.). Polity.
Silva, G. A. D., & Higuera, C. (2021). Political theology and COVID-19: Agamben's critique of science as a new "pandemic religion." *Open Theology, 7* (1), 501–513. https://doi.org/10.1515/opth-2020-0177
Singer, P. (1980). *Practical ethics*. CUP.
Singer, B. J., Thompson, R. N., & Bonsall, M. B. (2021). The effect of the definition of 'pandemic' on quantitative assessments of infectious disease outbreak risk. *Scientific Reports, 11*(2547), 1–12.
Tunander, O. (1989). The logic of deterrence. *Journal of Peace Research, 26*, 353–365.
Ward, I. (2021). The law of bare life. *Legal Quarterly, 72*, 186–211.
Weiss, M. G. (2011). Reality, simulation and hyperreality: An essay on Baudrillard. *International Journal of Baudrillard Studies, 8*, 2.
Wittgenstein, L. (1958). *Philosophical investigations* (G.E.M. Anscombe, Trans.). Basil Blackwell.

CHAPTER 2

SEQUESTERED COSMOPOLITANISM: EXCEPTION OR NEW PARADIGM?

Marin Beroš

Institute of Social Sciences 'Ivo Pilar' – Pula, Republic of Croatia

ABSTRACT

Even before the global pandemic crisis, cosmopolitanism was regarded as 'a noble but flawed ideal'. A moral perspective, despite the efforts of theorists who worked towards cosmopolitan democracy, has little impact on the larger political landscape. After a full year of 'social distancing' that transformed our world, the question arises – what will happen to the idea that so strongly relies on human commonality, togetherness, and sociability if all those features are severely lacking in our everyday lives? Will this prolonged 'state of exception' redesign our society and our political arrangements in such a manner that the idea of cross-border solidarity becomes not just unattainable, but utterly unimaginable? Will the global society remain just a dream from some earlier, more naïve times? Or is it still possible to be a cosmopolitan, 'a king of infinite space', even when we are forcefully sequestered in our tiny nutshells? The chapter will confront this changing socio-political landscape in order to provide an examination of changes in the cosmopolitan idea in general – and probably to give a little hope for an uncertain future.

Keywords: Cosmopolitanism; global society; social distancing; solidarity; hospitality

The year 2020 will certainly be remembered as a challenging year in the history books. In addition to all the problems global society was already facing, such as environmental deterioration, war, famine, and widespread continental migrations, we had, and regrettably still do at the time this piece is being written, a global pandemic. Although the promise of experimental medications and immunisation does offer some optimism, we are yet unsure of how this 'global quarantine' could influence our communities in the long run. It is entirely feasible that its impact on our lives will last for decades, if not longer.

However, when staying at home and limiting our social interactions was the only sure method of saving lives, there was no need for the reflection on the long-term effects of forced isolation on our innate human sociability, work environments, or political communities. These and a number of other questions will eventually need to be asked and answered, even if they are not urgent right now. When the epidemic is finally over, will we accept these changes as 'the new normal' or will we demand, and actively work towards for a return to an earlier state of affairs in society?

One of the concerns that is (sadly) low on this priority list is cosmopolitanism. What will happen to the idea that so heavily relies on human commonality, togetherness, and sociability if all those features are now severely lacking in our everyday lives? If we are scared to leave our homes, what will become of the notion that so much depends on crossing predetermined borders, overcoming our limitations, and encountering others who are vastly different from ourselves? What will become of the concept of cosmopolitan law, a bright beacon of hope for the oppressed masses of the world who are 'prisoners of geography'? What will happen to the promise of global civil society and global institutions if national interests always take precedence over our feeling of human solidarity? In light of everything, these are clearly not the best of times to be a cosmopolitan.

To confront the issue, this chapter will reflect on the status of cosmopolitanism in contemporary society. The intention is to ascertain how this period of global quarantine will affect the idea that is reliant on inherent human gregariousness, on our everyday contacts, on our willingness to accept the other in our homes. Also, it will take note of our expedient retreat from the public sphere, the change in the private sphere that came about from the collapse of the two, and how cosmopolitanism can survive in this changed political landscape. Of course, this chapter's aims are obviously limited because it does not seek to offer a conclusive prediction about the trajectory of cosmopolitanism, particularly while these developments are still in progress. Hopefully, it will be sufficient for the chapter to simply raise the issues surrounding this subject, which do not appear to be high on the political agenda of the world.

In order to fulfil that purpose, the chapter will provide a short overview of the intellectual history of cosmopolitanism. Starting with its origins in the Ancient Greece, this history will especially focus on Immanuel Kant and his vital contribution to the idea's evolution. His political essays, especially 'Perpetual Peace', represent the watershed moment, as he was the first philosopher to discuss cosmopolitanism's ethical implications before applying his conclusions to issues pertaining to international affairs. In addition to bringing about a paradigm shift in cosmopolitan thought, he also made evident the issue cosmopolitanism is still facing today – how to establish a global civic society that would uphold peace? His solution to this problem was proposal of a new type of law, cosmopolitan law, which would be applicable both to states and individuals, that would be founded on universal hospitality. This early 19th century development still resonates heavily with modern day political cosmopolitanism, not only in the search for optimal global political arrangement, but also in the works of authors concerned with human (cosmopolitan) rights. This chapter is going to give stronger focus on the latter, by referencing the works of modern authors such as Seyla Benhabib and Jacques Derrida who made the topic of hospitality one of the central aspects on their thought on cosmopolitanism.

After providing this account of modern cosmopolitan authors, the chapter will suggest that, for all the nobleness of its aspirations, it seems that cosmopolitanism started losing its power earlier than our current crisis. And the explanation is straightforward – modern cosmopolitanism was not successful in confronting and solving the problems of our globalised world, as it was hoped some 30 years ago. The epidemic simply made its inherent shortcomings more problematic, of which four are identified in this chapter – cosmopolitanism's elitism, its Western origins, the level of demand it placed on an individual, and finally, the vagueness of the idea. Furthermore, we will be asking whether this development will alter how cosmopolitanism is perceived in the future. Is it possible to have 'sequestered cosmopolitanism', or cosmopolitanism with a condensed public sphere? Despite all its shortcomings, the chapter will finally indicate the positives of cosmopolitanism, with the aim of providing hope even in these challenging times.

Cosmopolitanism today is still primarily seen as an idea or a behavioural pattern endorsed by a specific group of people known as cosmopolitans or 'citizens of the world', rather than as a comprehensive concept incorporating moral, political, and cultural aspects that influence our societal and political arrangements. In order to better understand that remark, let me provide an analogy: whereas nationalism as a doctrine undoubtedly had an impact on the creation of contemporary nations, cosmopolitanism's influence, as its political opposite, has been, at least thus far, more modest. For instance, without the idea of cosmopolitanism to inform it, our present understanding of human rights would undoubtedly be greatly diminished; nonetheless, cosmopolitanism has had very little success in terms of its impact on the political ordering of the world. Our various international organisations contain a cosmopolitan kernel, but that kernel is often shadowed by a plethora of national interests. Finally, the idea of cosmopolitan law has been present for nearly two centuries, but it is still regarded as a 'work in progress' – a theoretical exercise for philosophers and jurists with negligible impact on international law practice.

Knowing the idea's antinomic roots, its minimal legal influence is scarcely surprising. The Cynic Diogenes of Sinope (Diogenes Laertius, 2018) first said, 'I am cosmopolitan!' but not with the purpose of becoming the first citizen of the world, but rather to express displeasure with the regulations of ancient poleis. His initial negative idea has been taken by the Stoic school and expanded it into a positive concept – that all humans are morally equal because of our capacity for reason, which enables us to perceive and revere the natural law that governs the cosmos. It should be highlighted that in the ancient world of slaves and their masters, the Stoic idea that all persons engaged in reason and hence should be valued equally was a difficult position to uphold. Even so, it appears that the school's founder, Zeno of Citium, was not a direct proponent of cosmopolitanism (Schofield, 1999). Zeno's notion of an ideal political society – a cosmopolis, city shared by sages and gods – was later developed by his pupil Chrysippus.

The subsequent development of the Stoic school adapted this ethical idea to the political demands of the time. Gradually, under the influence of Roman authors such as Cicero, the idea of human fellowship founded on shared reason developed into *ius gentium*, the law that governs the ties between imperial subjects. However, through merging with the Jewish mystical tradition, these Stoic ethical ideas had a significant impact on the development of Christianity. The concept of dignity, or the acknowledgment and appreciation of the divine in every human being, emerged from these elements. In turn, the pursuit of equality and justice that permeates Christianity influenced natural law theory, which had a significant impact on the formation, as well as the recognition, of universal human rights in the 20th century.

Following this initial stage in the creation of the concept of cosmopolitanism, this idea fell into 'the obscurity', which lasted until the 18th century. However, even though cosmopolitanism was not directly addressed, a sizable number of teachings still had an impact on how cosmopolitan thought continued to advance throughout this 'interregnum'. For instance, Dante Alighieri (1996) promoted universal monarchy in his 'De Monarchia', Erasmus (1989) of Rotterdam expanded on the teachings of stoic cosmopolitanism to advocate the ideal of world peace, and Hugo Grotius (2005) pioneered the concept of rights that a person has merely by virtue of being a human.

We can consider the beginning of 18th century as the conclusion of this 'obscurity' period, when interest in a new literary style – 'perpetual peace proposals' – arose (Aksu, 2008). The most renowned of these initiatives is Immanuel Kant's (1991) 'Perpetual Peace; A Philosophical Sketch', although he also addressed cosmopolitanism in the essay 'Idea for a Universal History with a Cosmopolitan Purpose' (Kant, 1991) and in parts of 'The Metaphysics of Morals' (Kant, 1996). In addition to making a turning point in the cosmopolitan thinking, Kant (1991) also clearly described the challenge that cosmopolitanism still faces today: 'The greatest problem for the human species, the solution of which nature compels him to seek, is that of attaining a civil society which can administer justice universally' (p. 45).

Kant used an already existing cosmopolitan ethical ideal to build a new type of interstate social contract in order to establish a 'civil society governed by common law'. To achieve this ideal, it was necessary to envisage a new type of law, which Kant refers to as cosmopolitan law. In contrast to international law, which imposes legal responsibilities on states based on conventions and accords, cosmopolitan law protects both the rights of states and the rights of individuals in their interactions with one another. In addition, Kant (1991) thought that mankind could only overcome its 'self-incurred immaturity' with individuals reaching their full potential by fostering a healthy global environment.

Additionally, Kant sees the state's existence as a method of ensuring the greatest possible individual's freedom, which he believes is the only innate right. However, states coexist in hostile conditions that need to be regulated in order for humanity to reach its full potential. In the absence of international order, states will run out of resources due to ongoing war preparations. Furthermore, Kant argues that a constant state of conflict between them will promote animosity towards residents of other countries, and thus erode people's moral integrity. Kant places such a high value on the external legal order as he believes that it is also vital for the internal structure of states. As a result, the formation of a worldwide system to administer international justice is necessary because local justice is dependent upon it.

In order to avoid a Hobbsian natural condition between nations, Kant presents six preliminary articles in his 'Perpetual Peace' that aim to limit the likelihood of war but cannot produce a lasting peace on their own, as well as three definitive articles that lead to lasting peace. These three articles propose that each country should adopt a republican constitution, that each country should participate in the *foedus pacificum* and that cosmopolitan right based on universal hospitality must be instituted. The alliance of states that Kant suggests should be a voluntary coalition with the primary goal of securing world peace, which, in turn, is beneficial for the realisation of all inherent human capabilities.

Now we shall turn to Kant's (1991) concept of cosmopolitan law, which he indicated in the third article – 'Cosmopolitan Right Shall be Limited to the Conditions of Universal Hospitality' (p. 105). The historical connection between the idea of hospitality and cosmopolitanism should be emphasised here. Both conceptions in their essence are subversive, unconstrained by the boundaries of existing political communities. Adherents of both concepts do not consider loyalty to any political community, whether it is a community of birth or one of choice, to be their primary – they owe higher loyalty to the more universal community of all human beings.

Kant follows in this tradition, believing that hospitality and cosmopolitanism are inextricably intertwined. According to him, universal hospitality is defined as a right to visit foreign territories and to be welcomed in them, because 'all men are entitled to present themselves in the society of others by virtue of their right to communal possession of the earth's surface' (Kant, 1991, p. 106). As our Earth is a globe of a finite shape, we must learn to coexist as 'no-one originally has any greater right than anyone else to occupy any particular portion of the earth' (Kant, 1991, p. 106). Therefore, no one can legitimately appropriate the surface while denying access to another.

However, the visitor's peaceful behaviour is a requirement for the right to universal hospitality. In that regard, cosmopolitan right is understood as a right to access foreign territory. No state can forbid foreigners from visiting it, and citizens of one state are free to attempt to contact people in other ones. Universal hospitality is likewise limited to the promise of starting a trade because it is not a right to demand actual trade. On the other hand, settling in foreign countries is a whole different problem. Kant is a fierce opponent of European colonisation of territories that were formerly inhabited by other people. Based on inequality in relations between the two sides, he condemns actions of oppression and exploitation of natives, and allows settlement on their territories only through a non-coercive conscious contract. He justifies his position by claiming that even seemingly unoccupied land can be used by shepherds or hunters and cannot be occupied without their permission.

Although his political and legal essays have traditionally been deemed 'minor works' with respect to his work on critiques, there has been an increasing number of disagreeing voices in recent years. For example, Pauline Kleingeld (2011) thinks that this short essay, written near the end of Kant's life, represents the culmination of his ideas on moral and legal matters. Whether or not we agree with her point of view, this article on international relations cannot be read in isolation without being linked to an analysis of cosmopolitan law and positioned within the context of Kant's moral philosophy. Kant's vision is fundamentally holistic, as David Heater (2002) has noted several times. Some writers, like George Cavallar (2007), even think that his entire cosmopolitan ambition can be misinterpreted if these links are not made.

Indeed, it is difficult to deny that Kant had a significant impact on modern cosmopolitanism, as he was the first philosopher to address the ethical aspect of cosmopolitanism and then apply the principles he established in that consideration to issues of contemporary international relations. However, focussing on his ideas about establishing a global civic society (as modern cosmopolitics does) isolates them from the intricate coherence of Kant's cosmopolitan thinking and provides an incomplete picture of the issue. Cosmopolitanism, according to Kant, is more than just politics; it also acts as a moral compass that points us in the direction of a system.

Kant's enlightenment ideas have become less fashionable in an era that considers itself postmodern, yet his goal of building 'a civil society which can administer justice universally' may still be seen as a sound idea. Even if we tackle this issue without respect for morality and from a purely pragmatic standpoint, it is terrifying to think of how much humanity loses every year because over two billion people live in 'unhappier' parts of the world, where survival is on the verge of poverty and hunger takes precedence over concerns for science, the arts, or other people's well-being. However, it could be argued that Kant's cosmopolitical theories did have a tangible impact on the world through the creation of international organisations like the League of Nations and the United Nations in the 20th century, both of which share some constitutional similarities with his proposed *foedus pacificum*. Unfortunately, both organisations have proved to be unsuccessful, particularly in terms of achieving long-term international peace. Nevertheless, just through their existence (however flawed), the hope for the peaceful future of humanity persists.

The majority of modern supporters of political cosmopolitanism that Kant established can be found in the field of international relations theory. This theory aims to disentangle the cosmopolitan element from its political–philosophical, and in Kant's case, from the moral–philosophical foundation, in order to turn it into a science addressing the method of ruling power, or global governance. Although there are significant differences between them, modern authors who approach this topic from a philosophical perspective usually try to highlight the discipline's foundations. Some political cosmopolitans support a federal system with a globally spanning body of limited power, while others support a centralised world state of some kind. Others, however, prefer more constrained international political organisations that concentrate on strictly defined topics, like the UN Millennium Development Goals. Prominent philosophers who have contributed to discussions of the international political system, such as Daniel Archibugi and David Held, as well as authors like Jürgen Habermas, John Rawls, and Thomas Pogge, have carried on Kant's legacy.

Nevertheless, considering our overreaching theme of cosmopolitanism and the state of exception, we should highlight a couple of authors. In keeping with Kant's views, Seyla Benhabib is one of the academics who has significantly influenced the growth of contemporary cosmopolitan thought, particularly in relation to the cosmopolitan law. She sees cosmopolitanism primarily as a project of mediation between the universalism of ethical norms and the particularism of national legal systems. In this realisation of universal ethical norms, she considers the project of human rights to be decisive. Concentrating on human rights, Benhabib relies heavily on Kant's understanding of cosmopolitanism as a right to hospitality. However, as we live in a different era than Kant, and because globalisation processes have eroded state sovereignty, which has, in turn, weakened the civil rights of persons living in those states, cosmopolitanism of our own times must also be significantly different. As a result, Benhabib believes that the right to hospitality should apply not only in the context of a visit, as Kant understood it, but in certain cases should also apply to long-term settlement. In other words, states today have obligations towards displaced people and refugees that are very different from those towards tourists and immigrants.

Benhabib also points out that the Universal Declaration of Human Rights, which is our main tenet and the greatest achievement of the human rights doctrine, recognises the right to freedom in crossing borders – a right to emigrate, that is, to leave a country – but not a right to immigrate, that is, to enter a country. 'Yet the Universal Declaration is silent on states' obligations to grant entry to immigrants, to uphold the right of asylum, and to permit citizenship to residents and denizens' (Benhabib, 2006, p. 30). Despite the cross-border, cosmopolitan character of human rights, the Universal Declaration is still mindful of the sovereignty of individual states. Benhabib (2006) therefore disappointedly concludes that 'series of internal contradictions between universal human rights and territorial sovereignty are built into the logic of the most comprehensive international law document in the world' (p. 30).

Another author contemplating cosmopolitanism has touched upon Kant's cosmopolitan law and the concept of hospitality is Jacques Derrida. He explained his views on the matter in the essay named 'On Cosmopolitanism' in which Derrida goes so far to present hospitality as one of the basic building blocks of ethics. According to him,

> Hospitality is a culture itself and not simply one ethic amongst others. Insofar as it has to do with ethos, that is, the residence, one's home, the familiar place of dwelling, in as much as it is a manner of being there, the manner in which we relate to ourselves and others, the others as our own or as foreigners, ethics is hospitality; ethics is so thoroughly coextensive with the experience of hospitality. (Derrida, 2002, p. 16)

In this essay, Derrida focusses his attention on the concept of 'cities of refuge', as they have been referred to historically, which is the practice of providing sanctuary to people fleeing intimidation, persecution, and exile. He traces this lineage to the Hebraic traditions mentioned in the Bible. According to the Book of Numbers, God instructed Moses to establish cities that would serve as 'cities of refuge' or asylums, with the first six cities welcoming and protecting the innocent from 'bloody vengeance'. Derrida attempts to resurrect this concept of 'cities of refuge' by advocating both a duty and a right to hospitality, which goes beyond the traditional notion of hospitality. In his efforts, he draws on Hannah Arendt's analysis of stateless refugees after two world wars. In her seminal work, 'The Origin of Totalitarianism' Arendt (1979) recognised two great upheavals, the first of which was a progressive abolition of a right of asylum. Regarding this right, Arendt noticed that although it has survived two world wars and it had continued to exist in a world organised into nation states, it is still felt as an anachronism and principle incompatible with the international laws of the state. The second upheaval recognised by Arendt was a massive influx of refugees in Europe, which necessitated abandoning the classic recourse to repatriation or naturalisation. Derrida (2002) drawing upon her insights asks 'How can the right to asylum be redefined and developed without repatriation and without naturalisation? Could the City, equipped with new rights and greater sovereignty, open up new horizons of possibility previously undreamt of by international state law?' (p. 7).

Of course, with this analysis of the cosmopolitanism as universal hospitality, Derrida intended to critically address a specific context, namely France's relationship with *sans papiers*, or illegal immigrants. In his analysis, he located a double or contradictory imperative within the concept of cosmopolitanism. On the one hand, there is an unconditional hospitality by which we should offer the right of refuge to all immigrants and newcomers, but on the other hand, hospitality must be given under certain conditions. While he is aware that unconditional hospitality is difficult to attain, it nonetheless represents the desire behind the conditional hospitality that is necessary in our everyday dealings with others. He even notices that:

> At the time when we claim to be lifting the internal borders, we proceed to bolt external borders of European Union tightly. Asylum-seekers knock successively on each of the doors of the European Union states and end up being repelled at each one of them. Under the pretext of combating economic immigrants purporting to be exiles from political persecution, the states reject applications for the right to asylum more than ever. (Derrida, 2002, p. 13)

Apparently, according to Derrida, all the political difficulty surrounding immigration consists of negotiating between these two imperatives of conditional and unconditional hospitality. Finally, after identification of this contradictory logic at the heart of the concept, Derrida's (2002) solution is simple – 'experience and experimentation thus' (p. 23). He imagines that the experience of the cities of refuge will give rise to reflection on the questions of asylum and hospitality – and for a new order of law and democracy to come and be put to the test.

As it can be evidenced from these teachings, cosmopolitism (and cosmopolitics) certainly was not unimportant theoretical development in the global politics and international law. And yet, there never was a political party that considered its programme to be cosmopolitan, backed a cosmopolitan agenda or proposed cosmopolitan ethic as a means to resolve the problems in international relations. There never were courthouses that upheld the cosmopolitan law, nor universities to teach it. There are no truly cosmopolitan institutions present in our society, and finally, there is no global civil society on which those institutions could be founded on. The number of 'citizens of the world' may be rising, but they still do not constitute the cosmopolitan demos.

Therefore, if 'cosmopolitan ordering of the world' was never even present, can we truly consider that the COVID-19 pandemic represented a 'state of exception', at least in the sense that Giorgio Agamben (2005) following the concept of how Carl Schmitt understands it? Cosmopolitan law is a theoretical construct, therefore can we say that its 'suspension' provoked by the pandemic represents a state of exception? The answer is both yes and no. No, of course, as no written laws were suspended, and yes because we can claim that certain aspects of cosmopolitan teachings have become so ingrained in international relations practice that we could consider their lack as a breach of customary law.

But is the break in the steady development of global cosmopolitics truly a consequence of our 'new normal'? Did nations reclaim their sovereign authority in the name of security and infringe on our civil freedoms, or were there other forces at play, and we are unable to point to a specific incident that could have caused such a break? By shifting our attention to the period before the outbreak of the pandemic, it becomes apparent that the cosmopolitanism revival that began in the 1990s was already starting to lose steam. Three decades ago, with the fall of the Soviet Union and the subsequent conclusion of the Cold War, the shift from a bipolar to a unipolar political globe brought hope that the globalised world could be peaceful and democratic in some form.

Even though this assumption produced a rush of academic discussions about global democracy and reignited interest in the antiquated idea of cosmopolitanism, real politics is something fundamentally different, and the gap between the two became quickly apparent. If there was any 'global political optimism' in the 1990s, it now appears to be utterly gone. And this 'loss of faith' is evident even in the most ardent supporters of cosmopolitanism. The subtitle of Martha Nussbaum's (2019) book *The Cosmopolitan Tradition: A Noble but Flawed Ideal*, published in 2019, sums up the current sentiments on cosmopolitanism.

What are the properties that make cosmopolitanism flawed and unattractive to a larger portion of human race? There are several common complaints that render it 'unsuitable' for widespread adoption. To begin with, cosmopolitanism is usually perceived as an elitist outlook. The fact that its loudest proponents are primarily from the most privileged strata of world society may explain why the statement 'belonging to the world' is still perceived as 'unnatural'. Those who possess power and wealth do not need (civil) rights. To these people, which Craig Calhoun (2002) names 'a class of frequent flyers', their material and social position allows them to easily cross the boundaries which represent the obstacles for most of us, and as a result allow them to feel at home everywhere (or maybe nowhere?). On the other hand, migrants, although they are also crossing borders and denying attachments to the political community that was assigned to them by birth, are hardly seen as cosmopolitan, even though they do show similar qualities.

Another complaint that accompanies modern cosmopolitanism is that its foundation is distinctly Western. It belongs to the Western tradition of liberal thought historically, philosophically, and culturally. Because of this connection, cosmopolitanism in the rest of the world can be seen as a continuation of liberal policies applied internationally, making it foreign and incomprehensible, or perhaps even hostile and imperialist, which will eventually lead to its rejection. From this point of view follows the critique in which cosmopolitanism is understood as a highly individualised, almost egotistical political conception. As this is a complaint that dates back to at least the 19th century, it is not uncommon to encounter a contention that cosmopolitans are treacherous or at least unreliable citizens of nation-states. Furthermore, it should be noted that other civilisations have similar universalist concepts (e.g. Islamic – Umma and Chinese – Tianxia) that could be used to inform and transform cosmopolitanism.

Further complaint is that cosmopolitanism, taken as a moral doctrine, is extremely demanding on the individual. Cosmopolitans should always act on the premise that political boundaries should never limit our ethical judgments and decision-making. Our duty to help everyone is not diminished when our acquaintances or fellow citizens are not involved, nor it is strengthened when they are. Furthermore, cosmopolitanism demands that we consider both our relationships with our loved ones and those with total strangers equally. In a way, this stronger moral cosmopolitan concept is extremely counterintuitive, which is why proponents of nationalistic doctrine still have an 'upper hand', and we live in a political world that is still moulded on nationalistic principles in which the basic political unit is national state.

And as the final complaint to contemporary cosmopolitanism, we could offer its vague meaning, its lack of clear definition. Indeed, we are aware of modern cosmopolitanism in a variety of forms – as an idea of universal recognition of the moral equality of all people, as a project to establish a global political community, but also as a way of life associated with enjoying the cultural diversities. This ambiguity in the definition of cosmopolitanism is the result of the merging of several different idea-units into what we consider today to be the corpus of the idea of cosmopolitanism. This merging took place gradually, as these different ideological units developed in parallel with frequent intertwining and mutual influences for centuries, but despite the long duration of this process, it still had not produced a highly homogenised whole. Therefore, owing to its rich and complex history, cosmopolitanism is an idea that sometimes seems overly complicated, and for that reason incomprehensible to non-scholars.

Since it was unable to address a number of issues brought on by the collision of its intricate heritage with the realities of the modern world, it appears that cosmopolitanism may have lost much of its allure even before the global pandemic only made matters worse. If anything, our global quarantine clearly showed that the faith in the irreversible march of globalisation is misguided. The world that we know truly can fall apart in million (or about seven billion) pieces, but it needs a catastrophic event on a global scale. Unfortunately, we had one of those, and unfortunately, that event, that stop in the flight of globalisation's arrow had shown how fragile our communities really are.

In the end, new questions emerge – will this closing of the borders and general distrust between communities destroy cosmopolitanism? Will this prolonged 'state of exception' fuelled by the *raison d'état* redesign our society and our political arrangements in such a way that the idea of solidarity across the borders will become not just unattainable, but utterly unimaginable? Will the idea of global society founded on democratic principles remain just a cosmopolitical dream of some earlier, more naïve times?

At this historical point, it is hard to give a definitive answer, especially if we try to take the whole world into account. For now, we are sensing that our 'exodus to the digital world' will provide a significant change in the way we work, receive and provide education, and entertain ourselves, but this probably represents just the top of the list. It will take time for significant societal change to occur, and it is difficult to forecast its course. In terms of cosmopolitanism, this imposed isolation has a particularly negative impact on human interactions, which serve as the basis for both cosmopolitan theory and practice. The concept of hospitality, essential to most cosmopolitan philosophy, is reconsidered as relationships grow more 'virtual'. Can we still be cosmopolitans, 'kings of infinite space' if we are sequestered in our tiny nutshells? Or will we be haunted, as Shakespeare's Hamlet, by terrible dreams?

However, it is important to remember that cosmopolitanism has experienced both 'renaissance' periods, one of which was unquestionably the past 30 years, and periods of 'obscurity'. If the pandemic persists, it is quite possible that we will soon inhabit a different political environment, in which closed borders will become the new paradigm in international relations. But we should not be disheartened even if this turn of events comes true. Cosmopolitanism is not simply about crossing of the borders and denying the political arrangements we live in; it is also a state of mind. As a comforting note, it should be recalled that Immanuel Kant, probably the most important figure in the development of modern cosmopolitanism, rarely left his hometown of Königsberg. And yet he maintained the extensive network of contacts that allowed him to cast his gaze over the horizon. In a certain way, his example can give us hope. Even if we suffer setbacks in our cosmopolitan goals, it does not mean we should completely give up on them. After all, the idea of cosmopolitanism had shown its endurance through both good and bad times. One pandemic is not going to end it.

REFERENCES

Agamben, G. (2005). *State of exception*. The University of Chicago Press.
Aksu, E. (2008). *Early notions of global governance – Selected eighteenth century proposals for "perpetual peace"*. University of Wales Press.
Alighieri, D. (1996). *Monarchy*. Cambridge University Press.
Arendt, H. (1979). *The origins of totalitarism*. Harcourt Brace.
Benhabib, S. (2006). *Another cosmopolitanism*. Oxford University Press.
Calhoun, C. (2002). The class consciousness of frequent travelers: Toward a critique of actually existing cosmopolitanism. *South Atlantic Quarterly, 101*(4, Fall), 869–897.

Cavallar, G. (2007). *Kant's embedded cosmopolitanism – History, philosophy, and education for world citizens*. De Gruyter.
Derrida, J. (2002). *On cosmopolitanism and forgiveness*. Routledge
Diogenes Laertius. (2018). *Lives of the eminent philosophers*. Oxford University Press.
Erasmus, D. (1989). *The praise of folly and other writings*. W.W. Norton & Company.
Grotius, H. (2005). *The rights of war and peace*. Liberty Fund.
Heater, D. (2002). *World citizenship – Cosmopolitan thinking and its opponents*. Continuum.
Kant, I. (1991). *Political writings*. Cambridge University Press.
Kant, I. (1996). *The metaphysics of morals*. Cambridge University Press.
Kleingeld, P. (2011). *Kant and cosmopolitanism, the philosophical ideal of world citizenship*. Cambridge University Press.
Nussbaum, M. C. (2019). *The cosmopolitan tradition: A noble but flawed ideal*. Belknap Press.
Schofield, M. (1999). *The stoic idea of the city*. University of Chicago Press.

CHAPTER 3

CHECKS AND BALANCES IN TIMES OF PANDEMICS: THE PORTUGUESE EXAMPLE

João Cruz Ribeiro

Centre for Ethics, Politics and Society, University of Minho, Portugal

ABSTRACT

The purpose of this chapter is to present a brief overview about the measures adopted in Portugal in the context of the Coronavirus pandemic. This public health crisis gave room in two separate occasions for the declaration of a state of emergency. What is interesting, though, is that it can be argued that a real state of exception occurred not when the state of emergency was in force, but precisely when it was not. This has only been possible because the Government decided to adopt measures that would restrict fundamental rights, because the Parliament did not intervene in such a proceeding, and because the Administrative Supreme Court was arguably too lenient towards the Government. For a while at least, it seems to have occurred a 'provisional abolition of the distinction among legislative, executive and judicial powers' (Agamben, 2005). This has been confirmed by subsequent decisions from the Constitutional Court.

Keywords: State of exception; Coronavirus pandemic; public health administrative measures; judicial review, fundamental rights

1. INTRODUCTION

If exceptional circumstances demand exceptional measures, do they also demand exceptional Courts? The Coronavirus pandemic has allowed some interesting observations about how Courts, especially Superior Courts, exercise their competence in times of exception.

The purpose of this chapter is to present a brief overview of the measures adopted in Portugal in the context of the Coronavirus pandemic. This public health crisis gave room in two separate occasions for the declaration of a state of emergency. What is interesting, though, is that it can be argued that a real state of exception occurred not when the state of emergency was in force, but precisely when it was not. This has only been possible because the Government decided to adopt measures that would restrict fundamental rights, because the Parliament did not intervene in such a proceeding, and because the Administrative Supreme Court was arguably too lenient towards the Government. For a while at least, it seems to have occurred a 'provisional abolition of the distinction among legislative, executive and judicial powers' (Agamben, 2005, p. 7). This has been confirmed by subsequent decisions from the Constitutional Court.

This is a complex claim that I will try to structure as follows. First, I will describe the Portuguese constitutional framework concerning the state of emergency and refer to the two periods in which it was in force; this did not represent a true state of exception, or so I argue. Second, I will examine some measures adopted by the Government outside the state of emergency under the perspective of the Administrative Supreme Court; in my opinion, this Court allowed the Government to act in disrespect of the legislative competence, as established in the Constitution, and therefore permitted the enforcement of a real state of exception. Third, I will refer to subsequent case law from the Constitutional Court that appears to conflict with the Administrative Supreme Court and, thus, may be read as supporting my claim. Finally, as a concluding remark, I will assess whether or not the mechanism of judicial review has proven useful in this context.

2. THE PORTUGUESE PRACTICE UNDER THE STATE OF EMERGENCY

As other contemporary Constitutions, the Portuguese Constitution that came into force in 1976 allows for the possibility of a suspension of fundamental rights. This can only occur in two different hypotheses which the Constitution defines as *State of Emergency* and *State of Siege*. In such cases, the President of the Republic has the competence to declare the existence of a state of emergency or of siege and to suspend the fundamental rights as a means to deal with the critical situation at hand. The President shall hear the Government before issuing his Decree which shall eventually also be signed by the Government.

Once declared by the President of the Republic, the declaration shall be authorised by the Parliament. On formal grounds, the Parliament is required to approve a *resolution* to authorise the President's Decree.

The suspension cannot last longer than 15 days (but it is renewable) and shall specify which, and to what extent, fundamental rights are suspended, according to a strict application of the principle of proportionality. Furthermore, some fundamental rights cannot be suspended, for example, the right to life, personal integrity, criminal defence guarantees or freedom of conscience and religion.

Once in force, the state of emergency or of siege will be executed by the Government, adopting the measures within the limits established by the President's Decree. Access to Courts shall also be guaranteed in any case.

This constitutional framework was put into practice in the context of the Coronavirus pandemic. In two different occasions, a declaration of the state of emergency was put into force: first, between 19 March 2020 and 02 May 2020 and second, between 09 November 2020 and 30 April 2021.

These two periods when the state of emergency was in force had a fundamentally conservative purpose: the underlying idea was to resolve the threat to the system in such a way that it could be restored to the *status quo ante* (Ferejohn & Pasquino, 2004, p. 210). But, when reflecting about the Portuguese handling of the Coronavirus pandemic, it seems more interesting to observe what happened outside these two periods of time.

It does not seem that the state of emergency is a fundamentally linear issue and should not be problematised. To the contrary, some interesting problematisation has taken place concerning the role played by the constitutional organs. It would be interesting, for example, to discuss whether, and to what extent, the Portuguese system could be included in the neo-roman model proposed by Ferejohn and Pasquino (2004, pp. 213–216). The Portuguese scholarship has so far avoided the details of the question (Lomba, 2020a, p. 34). I will also leave this issue aside but, in doing so, I wish to acknowledge a peculiar difficulty that may not be obvious: questioning the compatibility of a given regime with the so-called neo-roman model should probably need to take into account the concept of *freedom as non-domination* (Pettit, 1997; Skinner, 2012). That is, the peculiarities of the roman model may in part be the result of a concept of freedom that only recently has been pushed to the centre of the debate.[1] This has some consequences, starting with the nature of rights itself and whether we should accept their pre-political nature, as in the contractualist tradition (Pettit, 2014, p. 71). But the complexity of this topic deserves much more attention than I could give.

In any event, Ferejohn and Pasquino's framework is useful to understand the Portuguese system. These authors distinguish between a *constitutional model* and a *legislative model*. Within the latter, the emergency is handled by enacting ordinary statutes that delegate special and temporary powers to the executive (Ferejohn & Pasquino, 2004, p. 217). By contrast, in the *constitutional model*, the Constitutions contain provisions to grant exceptional emergency powers to some constitutional organs. In this regard, it is clear that the Portuguese system obeys the constitutional model (Lomba, 2020a, p. 34). As described above, the state of emergency is constitutively dependent on the intervention of three constitutional organs, that is, the President, the Government and the Parliament. It has been suggested that this recent empirical experience has proven that the state of emergency is actually the result of a dual normativism, that is, it is the result of normative acts adopted both by the President and the Government (Gonçalves, 2020; Lomba, 2020a, p. 33). The President's Decree is not simply a political act, but a normative one, providing 'the framework under which the Government will intervene' (Lomba, 2020b). This dual normativism relegates the Parliament to a secondary level of importance. This has been the object of some harsh criticism. Some authors interpret this state of affairs as a disrespect towards the constitutional balance of powers (Sanchez, 2021). In their view, the Government should have acted as the mere *executor* of actions previously approved by the Parliament and the President (Sanchez, 2021, p. 768).

I do not wish to enter this debate, but I find this general oversight useful for a different purpose. Irrespective of the opinion one has concerning that debate, it is fair to claim that the idea of time compressing, associated with Schmitt's concept of exception, does not occur here. As Feldman (2010) clearly explains,

> Schmitt collapses two different moments of decision in his famous characterization of sovereignty. [...] [F]irst, a decision that there exists an emergency of such magnitude that it warrants the suspension of law, and second, a decision concerning what particular measures should be taken to respond to the emergency. In discussions of 'Commissarial Dictatorship' in an earlier work, Schmitt kept these two decisions separate. [...] However, in *Political Theology* Schmitt's definition of sovereignty brings these two moments together as if they are one momentary decision [...]. (pp. 139–140)

The Portuguese example seems significantly different. Indeed, in general terms, the constitutional framework, as described above, was respected during the state of emergency by the constitutional organs.[2] The Constitution retained its character of fundamental norm. In other words, these circumstances probably do not qualify as *exception* in Schmitt's theorisation. Indeed, Carl Schmitt (2005) argues that '[w]hat characterizes an exception is principally unlimited authority, which means the suspension of the entire existing order. In such a situation it is clear that the state remains, whereas law recedes' (p. 12). The Portuguese system, as described above, is far from attributing *unlimited authority* to any given constitutional organ. It seems clear that the separation of powers is enforced throughout the process of declaring and executing the state of emergency, even if the model of separation of powers is different from regular, non-exceptional times.

In fact, the state of emergency is declared by the President, but needs to be authorised by the Parliament, and the Presidential Decree needs to be signed by the Government. Furthermore, the one who declares does not execute. Indeed, it is the Government's competence to adopt the necessary measures to execute the state of emergency. Moreover, the Courts remain competent to control the Government's activity, namely to assess whether the measures are within the scope of the Presidential Decree and whether they respect the principle of proportionality strictly interpreted. It is of course undeniable that the Government is competent, under the state of emergency, to inhibit the exercise of fundamental rights without direct and legitimising intervention from the Parliament, but it is also clear that the Government's action is restrained to a considerable extent. Finally, and most importantly, some fundamental rights cannot be suspended. This means that the limits to the state of emergency are not only of a procedural type, but also of a material one.

Therefore, these seem to be rather different circumstances from those described by Schmitt (2005):

> The precondition as well as the content of jurisdictional competence in such a case must necessarily be unlimited. From the liberal constitutional point of view, there would be no jurisdictional competence at all. The most guidance the constitution can provide is to indicate who can act in such a case. If such action is not subject to controls, if it is not hampered in some way by checks and balances, as is the case in a liberal constitution, then it is clear who the sovereign is. (p. 7)

In this regard, we should probably look at the state of emergency, as it took place in the two mentioned periods, as a *liberal constitutional exception*, that is, 'an essential component of a liberal constitutional – that is, a rights-protecting – government' (Ferejohn & Pasquino, 2004, p. 211). It is far from Schmitt's *decisionism*.

3. THE REAL STATE OF EXCEPTION: RIGHT TO FREEDOM, RIGHT TO FREE MOVEMENT AND FREEDOM OF ASSEMBLY

From a very different angle, this historical experience is highly problematic. I refer to the *regular*, as opposed to the so-called *exceptional*, period, that is, the period of time after the pandemic initiated and when the state of emergency was not in force. I claim that it was precisely outside the state of emergency that a true state of exception took place.

To further clarify my point, I intend to refer to three fundamental rights enshrined in the Portuguese Constitution: right to freedom, right to free movement and freedom of assembly. I have chosen these three examples for two reasons. First, it is self-evident that public health measures approved as a response to the Coronavirus pandemic affected these rights wherever they were adopted. Second, in the Portuguese case, these rights were the basis of intense litigation in Courts. This judicial debate constitutes, therefore, a helpful instrument to fully understand what was at stake.

As seen above, the state of emergency was declared twice, when the public health crisis was more severe. It is fairly obvious, though, that this crisis has required public health and governmental measures during the remainder of the time. Indeed, between May 2020 and November 2020 (i.e. after the end of the first state of emergency and before the beginning of the second one), the Government adopted some measures to generally prevent and combat the disease. This also happened after the end of the second state of emergency in April 2021.

Oversimplifying, the measures adopted outside the state of emergency affected the three mentioned fundamental rights in the following ways[3]: concerning the right to freedom, the Government imposed an obligation of confinement to everyone who had been in contact with an infected person. The range of the people involved varied over time. Regarding the right to free movement, the Government imposed restrictions on the circulation throughout the country. On many occasions, circulation was limited within the county of one's residence and, in other occasions, some counties were isolated. Concerning the freedom of assembly, the Government adopted measures that limited assembly to a given number of people, sometimes as few as ten. This is a truly simplified picture of the measures adopted by the Government because they varied considerably, depending on the circumstances of the material time they were designed for. Nevertheless, even if simplified, this captures the essentials of the interference with the fundamental rights at hand.

According to the Portuguese Constitution, however, except in the case of a state of emergency or of siege, any restriction of inter alia[4] these three fundamental rights can only take place by fulfilling the conditions established in article 18. For the present purpose, the most relevant of the mentioned conditions consists in having the Parliament intervening in such a procedure: on formal grounds, the restriction of a fundamental right shall always be based, directly or indirectly, on a law approved by the Parliament.

Notwithstanding, all the governmental measures at stake were contained in *Resolutions*, adopted under the *administrative competence* that the Constitution attributes to the Government. The questions arising from these circumstances seem obvious: do these measures constitute an interference with the scope of protection of fundamental rights? Can the Government enforce such measures through a *Resolution* adopted under its *administrative competence*? Or, would the Parliament's intervention constitute, in any case, a necessary condition to confer constitutional validity to those same measures?

The question was first submitted to the Administrative Supreme Court and only subsequently to the Constitutional Court. To fully understand the details, a brief description of the Portuguese judiciary system is necessary. Roughly speaking, the Portuguese system has two streams, each of which has a Supreme Court. The first stream deals with criminal and private litigation (commercial law, tort law, family law and so on). The second stream deals with Administrative and Tax law. Oversimplifying, the second stream is competent to review the Administration's activity, including the Government's. In this regard, it is for the Administrative Supreme Court, as a Court of first instance, to review the constitutionality and the legality of the measures adopted by the Government. Finally, the Constitutional Court is competent to review, on appeal, the constitutionality of the legal norms under discussion in particular cases.

We shall see that the Constitutional Court and the Administrative Supreme Court have adopted radically different understandings of this issue. I will start my analysis with the case law of the Supreme Court because, to my mind, it performed a decisive role in the creation of an authentic state of exception.

3.1. The Case Law of the Administrative Supreme Court

As mentioned before, the Administrative Supreme Court is competent to review, as a Court of first instance, the Government's *Resolutions* such as those adopted as a response to the public health crisis. The content of the *Resolutions* varied according to the development of the health crisis circumstances, but it is accurate to say that, with a stronger or weaker intensity, the *Resolutions* generally interfered with the three fundamental rights identified above: right to freedom, right to free movement and freedom of assembly.

Individual citizens have contested before the Administrative Supreme Court the constitutionality of the mentioned *Resolutions*, among other things, for lack of legislative legitimacy. In their view, the Government could not adopt measures which corresponded to a restriction of fundamental rights. The restriction would only have been legitimate if the Parliament had intervened. Interestingly, the debate before the Administrative Supreme Court focussed on the right to free movement and the freedom of assembly. As we shall see, the right to freedom was discussed in the other branch of the judiciary system.

The decisions delivered by the Supreme Court were taken in proceedings of an urgent nature. Moreover, these decisions were temporarily very close to the reality under examination. For these reasons, we cannot say that we had a sort of well-established or settled case law regarding this issue. In any event, it was possible to identify some consistency in the case law: the Supreme Court, notwithstanding the dissenting votes, consistently decided to support the Government's legal arguments and upheld the *Resolutions*. Hereby, we may identify three cases as the leading cases, given the length and profoundness of the reasons contained in the judgements, as well as the equally thoughtful dissenting votes expressed in those same decisions. As a matter of fact, many other decisions from the Court used these three leading cases as an argumentative basis. I, thus, refer to the Court's decision on 31 October 2020[5] and to two decisions delivered on 27 June 2021.[6]

The Administrative Supreme Court was arguably too lenient with the Government.[7] In general, it accepted the Government's arguments and upheld the measures therein adopted. The common argument relied on the existence of an uninterrupted chain of legitimacy: that is, although the measures themselves were enforced without the Parliament's intervention, in the Court's understanding they were under a chain or net of legal diplomas that were, one way or another, covered by the Parliament; thus, they are the end result of a democratic process that can always be traced back to a point where it acquires parliamentary legitimacy. I would like to state that this is problematic in two ways: first, the legal diplomas that constitute the mentioned chain of legitimacy may be themselves unconstitutional; second, even if those diplomas are flawless from a constitutional law point of view, it is hardly acceptable that they can support the adoption of measures interfering with fundamental rights, such as those contained in the Government's *Resolutions*.

3.1.1. The Chain of Legitimacy

The chain of legitimacy is normally said to be constituted by four legal diplomas. Three of them were approved before the Coronavirus crisis and have different scopes:

- Law 95/2019 establishes the general standards for the protection of health.
- Law 27/2006 establishes the legal regime for the protection of the civil population; it aims at preventing collective risks concerning catastrophes, as well as rescuing the population affected in such cases.

- Law 81/2009 institutes a system of vigilance concerning public health that aims at identifying risk situations, such as those concerning contagious diseases, and also regulates contingency plans to respond to states of public disaster.

It is unconvincing that these diplomas, despite having been approved by the Parliament, allow the Government to introduce restrictions on fundamental rights in the legal order. It is clear that, within the measures adopted for the protection of the civil population and the correspondent contingency plans adopted in cases of catastrophes or public disaster, a degree of interference with fundamental rights may be unavoidable. Imagine the case where an industrial factory releases some toxic gas into the atmosphere that should cause severe injury to the civil population in case of continuous inhalation. It is not disputed that public authorities (the Government, in the last resort) can interdict circulation in a given perimeter, and for a given period of time, so that the population avoids inhaling the toxic gases. It seems obvious that this constitutes an interference with the fundamental right to free movement, but it does not sound problematic. Indeed, this hypothetical prohibition of circulation was represented as a concrete reality by the Parliament, that *by law* authorised the Government to enforce it in case it becomes necessary. The day the Government puts such a measure in force, the legislative legitimacy can easily be noticed.

A fourth diploma is also called to argue in favour of the chain of legitimacy – Decree-Law 10-A/2020. This diploma was approved by the Government on 13 March 2020, two days after the declaration of a public health crisis by the World Health Organization. It contained *exceptional and temporary measures* that arguably constituted restrictions of fundamental rights. However, the Government could not, I submit, have approved such a diploma without violating the Constitution. It does not have the constitutional competence to, by itself and without the Parliament's intervention, restrict fundamental rights. This is all the more obvious as the Parliament felt the need, through Law 1-A/2020, approved on 18 March 2020, to *ratify* the Government's diploma and to give *retroactive effects* to this ratification. However, this is problematic for two reasons: first, the Constitution does not currently provide for any such form of ratification and second, a restriction of fundamental rights cannot have retroactive effects.

Therefore, the *validity* of this diploma is itself at stake here. The least the Court could have done would be to examine the compatibility of this diploma with the Constitution, answering the doubts as above identified, which were, in any case, part of the public debate at the time. Nevertheless, it failed to do so. It is then possible to argue, all in all, that this diploma did infringe on the Constitution, and that for this reason, an important link in the chain of legitimacy is legally void.

But even if this was not the case, that is, even if this diploma was valid, it would not legitimise, in any event, the Government to adopt the measures at hand. Indeed, the argument of the chain of legitimacy is sometimes used to refer to situations where a legal diploma restricts a fundamental right, but where the restriction needs to be executed in detail afterwards.

However, the chain of legitimacy is hardly acceptable when a non-legislative diploma introduces in the legal order, *ex novo*, a restriction of a fundamental right. And this is what arguably happened in the cases at hand. An example may help to illustrate this case. Let us imagine that the Parliament passed a law regulating the activity of groups of supporters of football teams. According to this law, before a football match starts, everyone who wishes to join this type of supporters' groups should only assemble in some places: for example, in places that local authorities find appropriate to guarantee that conflict with other teams' supporters is unlikely. Furthermore, supporters should enter altogether in the stadium, having previously followed an itinerary that local authorities once more found appropriate. It seems obvious that, in this roughly defined example, freedom of assembly and free movement are restricted. It is also obvious that the law cannot define all the details concerning these situations and it will be for the local authority to decide, on a case-by-case basis, how to organise the groups of supporters, by telling them where to assemble and which itinerary to take. Deciding the details, which, in fact, constitute the practical expression of the restriction of the fundamental right, is nothing more than the execution of the law, previously approved by the Parliament using its legislative competence. Here we have a well-established chain of legitimacy, given that the local authority's decisions do not introduce any *new* restriction in the legal order. Those had already been introduced by the Parliament. But this is very different from what happened with the Government's *Resolutions*. Indeed, those *Resolutions* introduced in the legal order, for the first time, restrictions concerning inter alia right to freedom, right to free movement and freedom of assembly. And it is hard to deny for an obvious reason: this pandemic is truly unique in many respects. The response to this problem obliged societies to adopt measures that almost no living human being had ever seen. It is almost non-sensical to argue that the response to this crisis could be given with pre-existing legal tools.

3.1.2. The Odd Cosmopolitan Argument

As I said, I believe that the Administrative Supreme Court was too lenient with the Government, and this will probably become clear once we analyse the case law from the Constitutional Court. But before that, it is probably worthwhile to pay some attention to a specific decision from the Supreme Court. Such a decision was delivered on 10 September 2020[8] on a case involving freedom of assembly: the prohibition of assembly in public places of more than 10 or 20 people (depending on the circumstances); this prohibition, contained in a Government's *Resolution*, was contested before the Administrative Supreme Court by an individual citizen. In this case, the Court took the initiative to include an additional argument capable of justifying the Government's action: besides the already well-known argument of the uninterrupted chain of legitimacy, the Court added that this chain of democratic legitimacy was reinforced by the *international technical internormativity*.[9]

What does this mean? The Court is not totally clear concerning this matter. It says that the measures at hand were adopted, on the one hand, according to the Recommendations from international organisations such as the World Health Organisation (WHO) and, on the other, in respect to the need for *almost simultaneous* actions by States in a globalised world. These two features, according to the Court, justified the integration of the national measures within the scope of *international technical internormativity*, but the Court falls short of a definition of any kind.

The idea of internormativity is intimately associated with the idea of legal pluralism, which according to a classical definition means *the presence in a social field of more than one legal order* (Griffiths, 1986, p. 1). Therefore, different sources of normative prescriptions establish relationships of competition, convergence, juxtaposition and conflict. When the Court refers to *international internormativity* it seems to be recognising the existence of a complex interaction between the national order and other community norms whose origins lay beyond the state. Furthermore, the Court calls it *technical internormativity*. Although this is not clear, the Court seems to be referring to the nature of the Recommendations issued by the WHO, which may be understood as technical. To my mind, the Court is establishing a difference between these Recommendations and, say, the European Commission's decisions to accept state aid for some airline companies in the pandemic context. Where the latter were political in character, the former correspond to a sort of scientific consensus according to the best information available; in that sense, I think, the Court considers that there is some scientifical objectivity in the WHO's Recommendations and it uses the concept *technical* to express it.

The upshot of all this, if I correctly interpret the Court, is that the Government's respect for the *international technical internormativity* reinforces the democratic legitimacy of the measures adopted. In other words, *international technical internormativity* can preclude the Parliament's intervention without affecting the democratic legitimacy of a specific restriction of fundamental rights.

The full implications of this idea would deserve much more attention. But a very brief comment is inescapable. The Court seems to accept not only a restriction of fundamental rights grounded on a very thin and poor, if any, constitutional support; the Court seems to willingly accept that a restriction of fundamental rights can occur to give satisfaction to normative demands that are technical in character and have originated in a non-constitutional source.

With all due respect, this seems blatantly unconstitutional. More importantly, this confirms the tendency of this Supreme Court to open the door for a true state of exception. I will return to this point in the last section.

4. THE QUESTION BEFORE THE CONSTITUTIONAL COURT

As mentioned before, the Constitutional Court took a very different stance. To an extent, the circumstances of the cases may have had some influence on this outcome.

Indeed, the Court has delivered three judgments on 1 February 2022[10] ruling that the Government's *Resolutions* violated the Constitution.

At the outset, it should be pointed out that these three cases originated in the so-called *common courts*, that is, the branch of the judiciary that deals with *inter alia* criminal law. A common feature of all these cases is the fact that they were originated in a *habeas corpus* petition. Indeed, in two of these cases, a minor student was notified by the public health authority to stay in confinement after a diagnosed case of Coronavirus infection occurred in the minor's classroom. This occurred within the legal framework defined by the Government's *Resolution* which attributed to the public health authority the competence to decide, and consequently to notify, who should remain in a situation of confinement. In the third case, a passenger arrived at a Portuguese airport and, because the flight originated in a country that at that moment was considered as representing a risk to public health, was ordered by the border authority to remain in a situation of confinement for a period of fourteen days.

In each of these three cases, a *habeas corpus* petition was submitted at the local criminal Court. In all cases, the local Courts ruled in favour of the applicants and decided that those orders represented an unconstitutional interference with the right to freedom. In fact, those interferences originated in the Government's *Resolutions* which had been adopted without the Parliament's intervention; therefore, the Courts continued, the Government had exercised a constitutional competence that pertained to another constitutional organ, that is, the Parliament. Indeed, such a sufficiently characterised interference with fundamental rights could only be enacted through the parliamentary legislative competence.

The local Courts had no difficulty in not applying the rules contained in the Government's *Resolutions* due to the disrespect of the Constitution. Why did all the three cases end up in the Constitutional Court? According to the Portuguese legal system, every time that in a specific case pending before a national Court such a situation occurs, that is, every time that a Court decides that a rule contained in a legal diploma breaches the Constitution, the Public Prosecutor office has a legal obligation to appeal to the Constitutional Court. This is a mechanism that intends to provide some uniformity regarding the application of constitutional law and avoids wide divergent understandings as to what actually infringes the constitutional text. In these cases, however, the rule at issue was not enshrined in a legal diploma, but in a *Resolution.* For that reason, appeal was not mandatory but optional. Considering the public concern and a wide debate about these measures, the Public Prosecutor office opted to lodge an appeal before the Constitutional Court.

Therefore, the Constitutional Court had the possibility to assess the constitutionality of the Government's *Resolutions*. In all three cases, it upheld the local criminal Court decisions. Interestingly, the Government had the possibility to produce written observations before the Constitutional Court. Using this possibility, the Government presented the *chain of legitimacy* argument. The Court, however, dismissed the argument. Analysing in detail all the legal diplomas that allegedly constitute the said *chain of legitimacy*, the Court demonstrated that they were all insufficient to properly support a restriction of fundamental rights.

Indeed, the Court found that the provisions enshrined in the Government's *Resolutions* constituted a sufficiently characterised restriction of that fundamental right – the right to freedom; they constituted therefore a deprivation of freedom. But the Court went as far as declaring that any measure capable of affecting the scope of some fundamental rights could only be enforced through the exercise of the Parliament's legislative competence. That is, it is not only hard-core restrictions on fundamental rights that should necessarily be approved in the mentioned circumstances, but *any* measure or rule concerning the regime of those fundamental rights should be submitted to the Parliament's intervention.

This seems to be in direct conflict with the case law from the Administrative Supreme Court. Unfortunately, none of the applicants before the Administrative Supreme Court has appealed to the Constitutional Court.

5. CONCLUDING REMARKS

In the precedent sections, I tried to summarise the case law from the Constitutional Court and the Administrative Supreme Court. These two Courts, I think, decided generally the same questions in essentially conflicting directions. The basic question consisted in interpreting the argument of the chain of legitimacy. This is a well-known doctrine in constitutional law. But it seems that the Administrative Supreme Court has stretched it beyond its limits. Old bottles rarely resist new wine.

This leads me to conclude that an effective state of exception occurred in Portugal. This has happened, not through the *suspension* of some constitutional provisions, namely those concerning the protection of fundamental rights. On the contrary, it has happened *in times of apparent normality*, during which the Constitution was fully enforceable. In this regard, I conclude that right to freedom, right to free movement and freedom of assembly were subject to a *decisionist* behaviour by the Government, outside the realm of constitutional law. This is not infirmed by the fact that the Constitutional Court, once called to do so, has decided as described above. Indeed, the Constitutional Court's decisions are limited to those specific proceedings. Many more people have seen their right to freedom curtailed without any kind of remedy applied to their situation.

And this happened in a constitutional system that not only provides for judicial review, but that as a matter of fact has a Court of law whose competences are directed to the control of the Government's action. This notwithstanding, on several occasions the Government had the possibility to restrict fundamental rights against the rule of democratic deliberation, that is, without the Parliament's intervention. In this regard, attention should be paid to the role performed by the Administrative Supreme Court. At the end of the day, this Court's action contributed decisively towards this outcome, precisely due to its leniency regarding the Government. It has found legislative legitimacy in governmental measures, providing too much margin of manoeuvre in an area where the Constitution seems to be much more restrictive.

To an extent, the case law from the Administrative Supreme Court reinforces the argument of those authors who tend to be sceptical to the idea of judicial review. Indeed, against this background, it is hard to deny that 'the courts have proved unreliable protectors of individual rights in such circumstances' (Bellamy, 2007, p. 250). It is, of course, exact to say that this same legal system provided for a limited remedy, and that, when assessed by the Constitutional Court, the governmental measures were put to a more restrictive test. But this is probably too weak a compensation. And should lead us to a harsh conclusion: a situation of exception has occurred and, to a large degree, the judicial review proved to be ineffective.

NOTES

1. But that, interestingly, may have been at the centre of the discussion at the initial stage of American Constitutionalism (Pettit, 1997, pp. 33–35).
2. I am ignoring a rather relevant detail: in the first declaration of the state of emergency, the President of the Republic committed what was perhaps a technical mistake: the first declaration did not suspend the right to freedom (article 27 of the Portuguese Constitution) and therefore, the Government could not put into effect a general lockdown (as it did). The declaration suspended the right to free movement, but it seems beyond dispute that this was not sufficient to enforce a general lockdown (Reis Novais, 2020, p. 113). It is clear, nevertheless, that the President of the Republic wanted to create the constitutional circumstances that would legitimise a general lockdown and that the non-inclusion of the right to freedom in the catalogue of the suspended rights was not intentional. This was corrected in the declaration for the second period, which already included the right to freedom in the catalogue.
3. I do not intend to be exhaustive here. That work has been done thoroughly (Violante & Lanceiro, 2021).
4. To be accurate, I need to make reference to a distinction within the fundamental rights' constitutional regime. The Portuguese Constitution contains a catalogue of fundamental rights, which is divided into two parts. The first part refers to *rights, freedoms and guarantees* that correspond to, roughly speaking, civil liberties and political rights. The second part refers to *economic, social and cultural rights*. The special protection provided for in article 18 of the Constitution is only applicable to rights within the first category – those that are listed in the first part of the catalogue as well as those which are considered to have an analogous nature. Therefore, when analysing the regime established by article 18, reference should not be made to fundamental rights as these cover a broader concept. *Rights, freedoms and guarantees* would be preferable. However, I am afraid that using an alternative terminology would be too confusing. Moreover, all the three rights that I refer to in the text – right to freedom, freedom of movement and freedom of assembly – are included in the first part of the catalogue and, therefore, are especially protected by the regime established in article 18. In this regard, even if subject to criticism from a strict Portuguese constitutional law perspective, I will simplify and adopt the broader concept of *fundamental rights* in the text.
5. Proceedings 0122/20.1BALSB. Given that the decisions were anonymised and the parties' names were omitted, I will refer to the decisions using the number given to the proceedings.
6. Proceedings 085/21.6BALSB and proceedings 086/21.4BALSB.
7. To be fair, reference should be made to a dissenting vote expressed in each one of these three cases. The same Justice lucidly explained that the Government's measures were not legitimate and the chain of legitimacy argument should not be upheld. However, the majority felt differently in all cases.
8. Proceedings 088/20.8BALSB.

9. I stress that the Court took the initiative to include this argument to highlight the creative effort the Court introduced in its judgement. Indeed, this argument was not brought to the Court's attention by the defendant in the proceedings. Moreover, the Court clearly acknowledges that this argument cannot be directly read in the constitutional text. Furthermore, the Court does not mention any constitutional rule or constitutional principle from where this argument could be inferred. Finally, the Court makes no reference to previous decisions or doctrinal opinions in support of this argument. It is as original as it could be: the Court said what it meant and meant what it said.

10. Decision 88/2022, decision 89/2022 and decision 90/2022.

11. As usual in Portuguese Court's official websites and printed publications, the decisions are anonymised and the parties' names are omitted. For that reason, reference is made to the number given to proceedings. This article is based on the Portuguese case-law as it stood in February 22, 2022.

REFERENCES

Agamben, G. (2005). *The state of exception*. The University of Chicago Press.
Bellamy, R. (2007). *Political constitutionalism: A republican defence of the constitutionality of democracy*. Cambridge University Press.
Feldman, L. C. (2010). The banality of emergency: On the time and space of 'political necessity'. In A. Sarat (Ed.), *Sovereignty, emergency, legality* (pp. 136–164). Cambridge University Press.
Ferejohn, J., & Pasquino, P. (2004). The law of the exception: A typology of emergency powers. *International Journal of Constitutional Law*, *2*(2), 210–239.
Gonçalves, P. C. (2020). *Abdicação parlamentar na emergência e continuação da abdicação na calamidade*. https://observatorio.almedina.net/index.php/2020/05/21/abdicacao-parlamentar-na-emergencia-e-continuacao-da-abdicacao-na-calamidade/
Griffiths, J. (1986). What is legal pluralism? *The Journal of Legal Pluralism and Unofficial Law*, *18*(24), 1–55.
Lomba, P. (2020a). Constitution, state of emergency and public health Administration: Some problems. *e-Pública*, *7*(1), 27–43.
Lomba, P. (2020b). *The constitutionalized state of emergency: The case of Portugal*. https://verfassungsblog.de/the-constitutionalized-state-of-emergency/
Pettit, P. (1997). *Republicanism: A theory of freedom and government*. Oxford University Press.
Pettit, P. (2014). *Just freedom: A moral compass for a complex world*. WW Norton & Company.
Reis Novais, J. (2020). Fundamental rights and unconstitutionality in a situation of crisis – Regarding COVID-19 epidemic. *e-Pública*, *7*(1), 78–117.
Sanchez, P. F. (2021). Sobre os poderes normativos do Presidente da República e do Governo em estado de excepção. *Revista da Ordem dos Advogados*, *81*, 755–805.
Schmitt, C. (2005). *Political theology: Four chapters on the concept of sovereignty* (G. Schwab, Trans.). University of Chicago Press.
Skinner, Q. (2012). *Liberty before liberalism*. Cambridge University Press.
Violante, T., & Lanceiro, R. (2021). *The response to the COVID-19 pandemic in Portugal: A success story gone wrong*. https://verfassungsblog.de/the-response-to-the-covid-19-pandemic-in-portugal-a-success-story-gone-wrong/

CASE LAW[11]

ADMINISTRATIVE SUPREME COURT

Judgement of 10 September 2020, proceedings 088/20.8BALSB. Retrieved February 21, 2022, from http://www.dgsi.pt/jsta.nsf/35fbbbf22e1bb1e680256f8e003ea931/6a509a0b01993cfb802585e600446990?OpenDocument&ExpandSection=1#_Section1

Judgement of 31 October 2020, proceedings 0122/20.1BALSB. Retrieved February 21, 2022, from http://www.dgsi.pt/jsta.nsf/35fbbbf22e1bb1e680256f8e003ea931/65cabfb083dcdc838025861b0039a6c8?OpenDocument&ExpandSection=1#_Section1

Judgement of 27 June 2021, proceedings 085/21.6BALSB. Retrieved February 21, 2022, from http://www.dgsi.pt/jsta.nsf/35fbbbf22e1bb1e680256f8e003ea931/09d52afaf37ce2de802587050057df33?OpenDocument&ExpandSection=1#_Section1

Judgement of 27 June 2021, proceedings 086/21.6BALSB. Retrieved February 21, 2022, from http://www.dgsi.pt/jsta.nsf/35fbbbf22e1bb1e680256f8e003ea931/67d271022f889b2b80258705006ba798?OpenDocument&ExpandSection=1#_Section1

CONSTITUTIONAL COURT

Judgement of 01 February 2022, decision 88/2002. Retrieved February 21, 2022, from http://www.tribunalconstitucional.pt/tc/acordaos/20220088.html

Judgement of 01 February 2022, decision 89/2002. Retrieved February 21, 2022, from http://www.tribunalconstitucional.pt/tc/acordaos/20220089.html

Judgement of 01 February 2022, decision 90/2002. Retrieved February 21, 2022, from http://www.tribunalconstitucional.pt/tc/acordaos/20220090.html

CHAPTER 4

FINLAND AND THE COVID-19 PANDEMIC — RISKS INHERENT IN A RESTRAINED STATE OF EXCEPTION

Tatu Hyttinen[a] and Saila Heinikoski[b]

[a]*University of Turku, Finland*
[b]*Finnish Institute of International Affairs, Finland*

ABSTRACT

The rule of law has been tried in many countries under the state of exception during COVID-19. This chapter focusses on the case of Finland, the only Nordic country to declare a state of exception during the pandemic. Drawing from theoretical accounts on the state of exception, it analyses to what extent the Finnish democratic Rechtsstaat *has coped in the state of exception.*

The authors propose the concepts of a radical and restrained state of exception and argue that while the Finnish states of exception were rather restrained than radical, there are risks involved in the fact that powers granted by the Emergency Powers Act to be used during a state of exception are moved to normal legislation. Indeed, as Giorgio Agamben, among others, has warned, the state of exception may become permanent and undermine democracy and the rule of law. The chapter provides a dialogue between theory and empirics related to a state of exception, applying theoretical insights on the case of Finland during COVID-19.

Keywords: Finland; fundamental rights; state of exception; rule of law; COVID-19

INTRODUCTION

The rule of law has been tried in many countries under the state of exception during COVID-19. This chapter analyses the state of exception from the perspective of Finland, the only Nordic country that declared state(s) of exception in the pandemic. The research question is the following: *to what extent has the Finnish Rechtsstaat coped in the states of exception spurred by COVID-19?* In the analysis, we move between the fields of philosophy, jurisprudence and political science, and our primary interest is to apply theoretical accounts on the state of exception to an empirical analysis. Hence, our aim is not to describe in detail the states of exception but to consider what the states of exception have revealed about the resilience and possible problems related to the rule of law in Finland.

We start this chapter with two sections that provide background for the later theoretical and empirical discussions. In the first section, we describe the history and current state of the Finnish rule of law development. In the second section, we introduce the concepts of a radical and restrained state of exception, which we have developed on the basis of theoretical debates on the topic. The section that follows briefly concretises the restrictions to fundamental rights realised during the states of exception in Finland. Thereafter follows a discussion, in which we assess the Finnish practices on the basis of the presented restrictions and the theoretical accounts. The final section provides conclusions on the problems of a restrained state of exception and resilience of the rule of law in Finland.

THE DEVELOPMENT OF THE FINNISH *RECHTSSTAAT* INTO A MATURE DEMOCRATIC *RECHSSTAAT*

Conceptual limits can be set for a *Rechtsstaat* (see e.g. Ferrajoli, 2007; Hallberg, 2004). First of all, the division of powers requires the state to separate between legislative power, executive power and judicial power. In addition, the state shall be organised with legal rules, the legislation shall be equally binding for all people, public power shall be based on law and courts shall be independent. After the Second World War, a conception that fundamental rights need to be respected in a *Rechtstaat*, also started to gain weight. Nowadays, a *Rechtsstaat* fully respecting fundamental rights can be called a democratic *Rechtsstaat*. The intention has been to emphasise that the rule of law not only relates to law and legality (*Rechtsstaat*), but equally to substantive righteousness filtered through fundamental rights (democratic *Rechtsstaat*) (Ferrajoli 2007, p. 323). Fundamental rights, indeed, have become the value basis that each state considering itself a *Rechtsstaat* must commit to (Hallberg, 2004; Hyttinen, 2015, p. 37; Lagerspetz, 2002, p. 41; Tuori, 1992).

We have no reason to assume that a democratic *Rechtsstaat* would be the endpoint of the *Rechtsstaat* development. During our times, the criteria for a democratic *Rechtsstaat* that respects fundamental rights have, however, become the measure with which the rule of law of states is assessed. When measuring the rule of law, Finland has become one of the countries with the highest rule of law index in the world (e.g. WPJ Rule of Law Index, 2021, where Finland was ranked third). A central factor in this development is probably the fall of the Berlin Wall (1989), as a result of which Finland, first, joined the Council of Europe (1989), thereby implementing the European Convention on Human Rights (1990). After this, a reform of fundamental rights was realised (1995), Finland joined the European Union (1995) and the Constitution was completely reformed in 2000 (Heinonen & Lavapuro, 2012, p. 7). This development was spurred by the fall of the Soviet Union and the end of the division of Europe, which also meant end for the so-called Finlandisation period (Blomberg, 2011; Puumalainen, 2018, pp. 155–159). The question was not only of major foreign policy changes, but equally about Finnish leaders wanting to also legally emphasise their commitment to Western values, which in practice meant strong commitment to fundamental and human rights in legislation, activities of public officials and legal praxis. In this regard, one has discussed the Europeanisation of the Finnish legal culture (Heinonen & Lavapuro, 2012), which has referred to how the Finnish *Rechtsstaat* matured from a strong *Rechtsstaat* into a genuine democratic *Rechtsstaat*.

In hindsight, the last decade of the 20th century impacted the maturity of the Finnish *Rechtsstaat* more than any decade in the Finnish history. Still, it was not a question of the country suddenly becoming a mature democratic *Rechtsstaat*, but the maturing started almost a quarter of a century before, during which the criteria for the rule of law started to be conceived in Finland in a new manner. If mainly law and legality were emphasised still in the early 1990s, the 21st century requires that also fundamental rights are fully respected in legislation and in legal praxis. The rule of law development is interestingly also reflected in the Finnish legal literature, where argumentation with fundamental rights has become the main rule instead of exception during the past 25 years, which has also accelerated the fact that the Finnish legal culture and legal debate have started to focus more on fundamental rights (Länsineva, 2011, pp. 339–355; Nuotio, 2020, pp. 1236–1249, especially p. 1248). Finland's rapid maturing into a democratic *Rechtsstaat* that respects fundamental rights can be accounted by many factors, such as strong tradition of legality and appropriate political institutions, which had become functional already before the fall of the Berlin Wall.

The fast positive development should not be criticised, on the contrary. There is, however, a problem involved in the pace: Finland does not enjoy historical depth as a democratic *Rechsstaat*, at least in the sense that fundamental rights would have gained full weight in legislation or legal praxis.[1] Hence, COVID-19 has provided a test for analysing how strong the Finnish *Rechtsstaat* is in crisis situations. Indeed, historically, different types of states of exception have revealed something essential about the resilience of the rule of law.

RADICAL AND RESTRAINED STATE OF EXCEPTION

An existential challenge for the existence of a *Rechtsstaat* has been posed by different crisis situations, in which the following question has been actualised: to what extent can a *Rechtsstaat* compromise its central principles without losing its status as a *Rechtsstaat* (Lagerspetz, 2002, pp. 39–60)? This is not a new question; the state obligation to comply with the law in crisis situations was already examined both in ancient Greece and in the Roman Empire, as illustrated by one of the most famous theorists on the state of exception, Giorgio Agamben (Agamben, 2005, pp. 41–51; see also Lagerspetz, 2002, pp. 43–44). The discussion is known as philosophy on the state of exception (*Ausnahmezustand*), to which, in addition to philosophers, several political scientists and constitutional scholars have contributed (Cornell & Salminen, 2018; Edgell et al., 2021; Győry & Weinberg, 2020; Heupel et al., 2021; Jyränki 1989; Tuori, 1992).

The discussion has been characterised by its theoretical nature but also by the fact that it has been closely connected with social reality. Historically, the state of exception has been discussed during times of crisis, while during more peaceful times, questions regarding the state of exception have not received similar attention (Lagerspetz, 2002, p. 46). For example, during the wars at the beginning of the 20th century, the debate was vivid (the most famous examples of wartime theorists include Carl Schmitt and Walter Benjamin, see Benjamin, 2003; Schmitt, 2005), while there has been less debate in the second half of the century, when the circumstances at least in the Western world were more peaceful despite of the Cold War. For example, the key political and legal theorists of the 20th century (such as John Rawls, Jürgen Habermas and Ronald Dworkin) have not (as far as we are aware) examined issues related to the state of exception to the extent their predecessors did in the 20th century. As a result of COVID-19, questions related to the state of exception have again found their place in the writings of legal scholars and social theorists (e.g. Agamben, 2020; De Angelis & De Oliveira, 2021; Győry & Weinberg, 2020; Heupel et al., 2021; Kipfer & Mohamud, 2021). Judging by the contemporary debate, Schmitt, Benjamin and Agamben can be considered the most authoritarian theorists on the state of exception, the accounts of whom are summarised in Table 4.1.

Regardless of the theoretical commitments, the basic logic and core problem of the state of exception can be summarised as follows. First, a state enters into a crisis that requires fast reaction. It can be a question of a war but also, for example, of a rapidly spreading contagious disease whose controlling requires restricting people's fundamental rights. Since the situation is new and acute, its parliamentary management through legislation is too slow. Hence, the executive power (the government) finds an interest in disregarding the tripartite division

Table 4.1. The Relation Between the State of Exception and the Rule of Law in the Writings of Benjamin, Schmitt and Agamben.

	Schmitt	Benjamin	Agamben
State of exception	A state of exception justifies undermining democracy and rule of law	A fictitious state of exception is the rule undermining democracy and rule of law	Permanent state of exception is a technique of government to alter the separation of powers

of power and starts governing with decrees. Decrees have the force of law, that is, they obligate citizens and authorities as strongly as acts. The grounds for providing decrees may be noble, such as safeguarding citizens' life and health, but decrees can also be abused. For example, they can be used to limit the rights of the opposition or to violate unjustifiably the fundamental rights of certain people and groups. At its extreme, the state of exception thus includes the risk of a dictatorship, which is reflected, for example, in the oft-quoted Schmitt's (2005) notion of the sovereign: 'sovereign is he who decides on the exception' (p. 5).

In its most radical and traditional form, a state of exception is a situation where the government ignores or revokes the entire legal justice system without law. The aim may genuinely be to protect the legal public order during wartime. However, the consequence is a state of unlawfulness, that is, the state which was meant to be evaded by declaring the state of exception. This creates the paradox of a radical state of exception: the state of exception dismantles the legal public order and justifies it with the need to protect the legal public order (e.g. Agamben, 2005, pp. 50–51). The most radical form of a state of exception means complete unlawfulness. For example, the constitution may as such aim at regulating the preconditions of a state of exception and the principles to follow during a state of exception, but nothing guarantees that a future crisis is adaptable to the predetermined acts, no matter how visionary the rules are (on the philosophical problems related to preparing regulation for states of exception, see Lagerspetz, 2002, pp. 46–51).

Indeed, in its most radical form, the state of exception is an exception from the legislation that regulates it; necessity knows no law, as Oliver Cromwell has famously stated. For a long time in history, it was even thought that discussion on the legal grounds of a state of exception is absurd (Agamben, 2005, pp. 41–51). The radical nature of the state of exception has received support from, for example, Rousseau's and Locke's social philosophical writings (on the conceptual history debate, see Lagerspetz, 2002, pp. 42–46), but in the First World War, many European countries (such as Belgium) practically operated in a radical state of exception (emergency laws), since the constitutions of the countries did not at the time include the legal possibility to declare a state of exception or introduce legislation on the state of exception (Jyränki, 1989, pp. 331–333).

In a more modern format, the state of exception is not considered as radical. For example, the states of exception declared during the COVID-19 crisis in different states have not meant complete ignorance of the legal justice system or that the states of exception would have been declared without being based on law (e.g. De Angelis & De Oliveira, 2021). The essence of the modern *Rechtsstaat* is based on the premise that the law includes the criteria for the state of exception and provides the government the authority to freeze some of the legal order. The state of exception and discussion thereon has become more constitutional especially during the last century, which has relativised the radical nature of the state of exception (Jyränki, 1989). The state of exception no longer means the comprehensive revoking of a legal justice system or freezing it, but lawful compromising of normal-time legislation. This is why we can discuss the states of exception becoming more restrained, the conceptual history of which can be traced back to the writings of Montesquieu (Lagerspetz, 2002, pp. 42–46).

This more restrained and constitutional form of the state of exception reflects the strengthening of the ideology of the state of exception. Hence, the development may appear ideal, but it includes a risk. As Agamben has noted, a restrained state of exception (though Agamben does not use this concept) does not mean radical changes, but in the big picture, everything continues as in normal times (Agamben, 2005, p. 18). Therefore, it is easier for the government to declare a state of exception and to maintain it. The question is not of a theoretical problem, because even restrained states of exception enable curtailing democratic rights and liberties.

States of exception becoming more restrained can thus be considered a risky path. It provides a manner to shift to the grey zone of the law, which often means restricting the fundamental rights of individuals or groups. One example is 9/11, which created a chronic state of exception in the USA (although it was not a state of exception in the traditional sense, see e.g. Scheppele, 2004). In the name of the war on terror, one started to justify permitting even torture, illegal prisons and preventing people from seeking justice with the need to protect from terrorism the free world committed to fundamental rights. The example is unrelenting, since the USA debate concerned, for example, the ban of torture, which is an absolute, that is, an inviolable right (see e.g. Article 7 of the International Covenant on Civil and Political Rights, ICCPR, and Article 3 of the European Convention on Human Rights, ECHR). In a similar vein, for example, the non-discrimination and the legality principle in criminal law are rights, the violation of which cannot be defended with any arguments. If a state violates absolute rights, there are no grounds to longer consider it a democratic *Rechtsstaat*.

The situation becomes more difficult when the violations in a state of exception concern relative rights. They are not absolute rights (although relative rights can also have an inviolable core, see Viljanen, 2001, pp. 229–250), but rights that reflect two social philosophy traditions: a liberalistic tradition emphasising individual rights and communitarian thinking based on Aristotelian tradition (MacIntyre, 1982; Taylor, 1994; Walzer, 1983). This is most clearly visible in the rights where one first safeguards an individual right and then defines on what basis the right in question can be restricted (Kortteinen, 1996, pp. 35–36). In a manner, the relative rights reflect the same historical debate that has been held on the state possibility to compromise its own obligations.

Relative rights are not anomalies but the most typical form of individual rights. A good example is the right to move freely, on the basis of which everyone is free to leave any country, including their own, but also to move within one's country. The right has been guaranteed in ICCPR (Article 12), ECHR (Protocol No. 4, Article 2) as well as in the constitutions of different states, such as in the Finnish Constitution (Section 9). The right is not, however, absolute, but the freedom of movement can be restricted by law if it is necessary in a democratic society for reasons of national or public security, in order to uphold public order, to prevent criminality, to protect health or morals or to protect the rights and liberties of other individuals (see e.g. ECHR, Protocol No. 4, Article 2(3)).

As visible, people's freedom of movement can be restricted, for example, for a health-threatening virus, which has been the case during the COVID-19 period

(Heinikoski & Hyttinen, 2022). Hence, it can be argued that currently also fundamental rights and derogations therefrom are only part of codified law and not political deliberation. The argument is not, however, convincing, if the issue is assessed from a theoretical perspective. Hence, it is unfounded to think that codifying the criteria for restricting individual rights in international conventions on human rights and national constitutions would increase the normativity of the restriction criteria – that is, decrease the possibility of the government to make arbitrary decisions when restricting people's fundamental rights (Hyttinen, 2015, pp. 9–10 and the references cited therein).

Fundamentally, it is a question of an existential problem related to normative decision-making, that is, any normative decision is subject to the justifications of the decision, which are subject to the justifications of the choice of the decision ad infinitum (Lagerspetz, 2002, p. 47). Hence, the decision to restrict a fundamental right has to be justifiable with grounds for decision, such as normative grounds g^1, g^2 and g^3. A critic can, however, ask how one can justify the decisive impact of the normative grounds g^1, g^2 and g^3. The response may be to refer to normative grounds g^4, g^5 and g^6 supporting grounds g^1, g^2 and g^3, but at some point, the endpoint of the norm regression must be considered a given (Lagerspetz, 2002, p. 47). Therefore, the choice of the decisive ground supporting the decision-making is ultimately a subjective decision that cannot be normatively captured, as Lagerpetz has – while writing on the philosophy on the state of exception – convincingly demonstrated (Lagerspetz, 2002, p. 47). This is why also restrictions to relative fundamental rights are decisions impacted by the values of the decision-maker.

Particularly problematic can be considered the necessity criterion included in international conventions, according to which restrictions to fundamental rights need to be necessary in a democratic society. Although not all rights include such restriction clauses, restriction clauses have *de facto* importance when assessing the possibility to restrict any relative right. These restriction criteria are, however, thoroughly political, although they are part of the codified human rights doctrine and constitutional tradition. We all have different opinions on how, for example, one should have regulated people's movement during COVID-19, the obligation to stay home or the right to go to school and work. A supporter of the rule of law can claim that in the end, the court (in Europe, the ECHR) will determine what is necessary in a democratic society. The argument as such is, however, in conflict with democracy (Hyttinen 2015, p. 120). If judges, such as those of the ECHR, were provided with the power to decide what (they think) is necessary in a democratic society, we would (in practice) live under a judicial dictatorship, instead of a constitutional dictatorship (on judicial dictatorship, see Tuori, 2003).

Since we refer to the freedom of movement as an example above, it should be emphasised that the freedom of movement is not a right that can be particularly easily restricted, but fairly many (individual) fundamental rights can be restricted in the same manner. For example, freedom of speech and the right to assembly are similar relative rights, that is, they can be restricted for several reasons, if the restrictions are necessary in a democratic society. Hence, even the most crucial political rights are subject to restrictions if that is in the interest of a democratic society – an interest whose definition in a state of exception is at the responsibility of the government.

The dangerousness of a restrained state of exception is, indeed, based on the fact that it provides the government the right to define what is necessary in a democratic society. This enables justifying compromises related to individual rights in a state of exception with normative argumentation, which alleviates the risk of abuse of power included in a state of exception. The logic is the following: first, a state of exception is declared, and the government receives the right to provide decrees with the force of law. Thereafter, the government decides what sort of restrictions to fundamental rights are necessary in crisis management and the decisions are justified by appealing to the criteria for restricting fundamental rights – in practice that the restrictions are necessary in a democratic society. Hence, even restrictions to fundamental rights realised in a state of exception are made to seem apolitical, that is, decisions whose acceptability can be deduced from the restriction criteria included in the doctrine of fundamental rights (more specifically on the criteria for restricting fundamental rights, see Viljanen, 2001). In reality, it is, however, a situation where the government has assumed the sovereign power to define what sort of restrictions to fundamental rights are necessary in a democratic society.

A good example is Finland, where even the restrictions to fundamental rights during a state of exception have been sought to be justified with normative argumentation. The argumentation is more fine-grained than above, that is, the legitimacy of the restrictions has been justified with the restriction criteria included in the Finnish doctrine of fundamental rights, such as by justifying restrictions with their precision, definition and proportionality (see Viljanen, 2001). Crucially, the question has been of the requirement of necessity, that is, that the restrictions have been claimed to be necessary in a democratic society (required by a weighty societal need). Restrictions that have been considered necessary during a state of exception, have, however, been necessary precisely from the perspective of the government (which has the right to provide decrees in a state of exception). This is most clearly reflected in the fact that the opposition parties have sometimes disagreed on the necessity of the realised restrictions, even though there was little contestation of the measures, especially in the beginning of the pandemic. Still, this does not lead to the conclusion that during COVID-19, the government would have acted in a manner that would deprive the status of a democratic *Rechtsstaat* from Finland.

Before assessing to what extent has the rule of law in Finland endured the states of exception during COVID-19, we briefly concretise the restrictions to fundamental rights realised during COVID-19-induced state of exception in Finland.

SHORT TIMELINE OF THE PRACTICES DURING THE STATES OF EXCEPTION IN FINLAND

The Finnish government faced an unprecedented situation when the COVID-19 cases started to rise in Finland in early March 2020. On 13 March 2020, the government and the president stated that Finland is in a state of exception and the government adopted the Emergency Powers Act 1552/2011 (Prime Minister's

Office Finland, 2020a). The state of exception ended after three months, on 15 June 2020. In spring 2021, the state of exception was again declared on 1 March 2021, ending on 27 April 2021.²

According to a background document of the decision on the first state of exception, it was declared in order to 'protect the public and guarantee its income and the country's economic life, maintain the legal system, fundamental rights and human rights' (Prime Minister's Office Finland, 2020b, p. 14). It was justified with the definition of the Emergency Powers Act of being a very widely spread dangerous contagious disease with impacts comparable to a particularly serious major accident. Typically, but also paradoxically, the state of exception declared in order to protect fundamental and human rights, severely restricted many fundamental rights.

On 17 March 2020, when the first state of exception was declared, several government decrees on the basis of the powers granted by the Emergency Powers Act were adopted (see Table 4.2). The government adopted a decree that took into use the provisions of the Emergency Powers Act concerning the management of social and healthcare units (Finnish Government, 2020e), and concerning the possibility to restrict the selling of medicine and other healthcare equipment (Finnish Government, 2020f). Under the Emergency Powers Act, the government simultaneously provided a decree on the right to extend the time limits for receiving social and healthcare services (Finnish Government, 2020b). Schools and day care were closed almost entirely for two months, and the government also provided a decree allowing derogation from the municipal obligation to organise day care and education (Finnish Government, 2020g). Finally, a decree concerning temporary derogation from annual holidays, working time and terms of notice was provided (Finnish Government, 2020c).

Some practices also required prior amendments in the normal legislative process in the parliament. Such was the closing of bars and restaurants that the government imposed with a decree on 31 March 2020. This serious restriction to the right to engage in commercial activity was considered to be in accordance with Section 23 of the Constitution as it would be temporary and possible only in a state of exception (Finnish Government, 2020a). The closures and restrictions with regard to restaurants and bars (and some other places, such as gyms and swimming halls) have been something that the opposition parties and the general public have mostly criticised due to their impact on entrepreneurs, workers and people who visit the places (see e.g. Hemmilä, 2021).

The most radical act of the government on the basis of the Emergency Powers Act, however, was the sealing off the Uusimaa region (region surrounding the capital with more than 1.7 million inhabitants). The government adopted a decree closing the region of Uusimaa from 27 March to 19 April 2021 on the grounds that it would slow down the spread of the disease in other parts of the country and thus secure the availability of intensive care in the entire country. The period was determined to end one week after Easter so that people from Uusimaa would not travel to their second homes elsewhere in Finland during the holiday (Prime Minister's Office Finland, 2020c). The government, however, repealed the decree already on 15 April since the situational picture illustrated that the closure was

Table 4.2. Restrictions and the Restricted Key Constitutional Rights During the States of Exceptions in Finland.

	Restriction	Restricted Constitutional Rights
First state of exception from 13 March to 15 June 2020	Possibility to obligate healthcare personnel to work	Freedom and rights of the individual (Section 1), the right to employment of one's choice (Section 18)
	Closing of schools and day care	Educational rights (Section 16)
	Restriction of selling medicine and other healthcare equipment	Freedom to engage in commercial activity (Section 18), Protection of property (Section 15)
	Closing of bars, restaurants and cafeterias	Freedom to engage in commercial activity (Section 18), Protection of property (Section 15)
	Sealing off the region of Uusimaa from 27 March to 15 April	Freedom of movement (Section 9)
Second state of exception from 1 March to 27 April 2021	Restricting the capacity and opening times of bars, restaurants and cafeterias	Freedom to engage in commercial activity (Section 18), Protection of property (Section 15)
	Centralising official communication to the government	Freedom of expression and the right of access to information (Section 12)
	Deciding on competent authorities in unclear cases	The rule of law (Section 2), freedom of expression and the right of access to information (Section 12)
	Direction of social and healthcare units	The rule of law (Section 2)
	Right to derogate from time limits in non-urgent treatment	The right to personal security (Section 7), the right to social security (Section 19)
	Retracted bill on restricting people's movement and obligation to wear a mask	Would have seriously restricted freedom of movement (Section 9)
	Delaying of the municipal elections from April to June 2021	Electoral and participatory rights (Section 14)

no longer necessary and such restriction to constitutional rights thus had to be immediately abolished (Finnish Government, 2020d).

The government held a meeting on 15 June 2020 when the state of exception was declared ended. It concluded that the pandemic could be controlled with normal powers. Furthermore, it stated that it has provided proposals on amendments to the Communicable Diseases Act, Healthcare Act, Social Welfare Act and acts related to medicine supply and education (Prime Minister's Office Finland, 2020d). This means that some of the powers that the government had used during the state of exception were moved to normal legislation.

On 1 March 2021, the background document for declaring the second state of exception stated that while vaccinations were already in use, the rate was considered too slow in order to cope without the Emergency Powers Act (Prime Minister's Office Finland, 2021a). The healthcare provisions were not considered immediately necessary.

However, declaring the state of emergency was argued to be necessary in order to be legally able to close restaurants and bars. In addition, Section 106 on centralising official communication to the government and Section 107 on deciding the competent authority in unclear cases were considered necessary by the government.

Spring 2021 also witnessed major debates on serious restrictions to constitutional rights, mainly concerning electoral and participatory rights as well as freedom of movement. The municipal elections were moved from April 2021 to June 2021 due to the epidemic situation, as the government proposal stated: 'A state of exception and elections can be considered a dangerous combination' (Finnish Government, 2021b, p. 7). The decision as such was not based on the Emergency Powers Act but processed as a normal legislative proposal in the parliament.

In spring 2021, the government was also preparing a major restriction to people's freedom of movement as they were considering restricting people's movement outside their home (and the obligation to wear a mask indoors and in public transport), but after critical comments from the parliament's constitutional committee, the bill was retracted (Finnish Parliament Constitutional Committee, 2021). According to the Constitutional Committee, the free movement restriction would not have only affected negatively the right to move freely but also the right to assembly, protection of private and family life, freedom to engage in commercial activity, religious freedom and educational rights, that is, the question would have *de facto* been of a decision simultaneously restricting several essential rights. Hence, the Constitutional Committee blocked the government proposal that would have allowed it to restrict people's movement with decrees, which illustrates that the government was not able to pass all envisaged restrictions, a sign of a functional democratic *Rechtsstaat*.

When the second state of exception was declared ended on 27 April 2021, the background memo stated that the only competence utilised under the Emergency Powers Act was the coordination of key communicative measures (Prime Minister's Office Finland, 2021b), which suggests that not all public authorities may have been able to communicate independently. This can be considered questionable from the perspective of functional democracy and freedom of speech.

In summary, the government availed of several provisions of the Emergency Powers Act but did not actually use all of the powers they granted.[3] Furthermore, it was not able to implement all the planned restrictions due to the existing checks and balances, such as the restriction to people's movement and obligation to wear a mask blocked by the parliament's Constitutional Committee. In addition to the ex ante control of the parliament, it has to be noted that even during a state of exception, it is possible to lodge a complaint for the Parliamentary Ombudsman and the Chancellor of Justice for restrictions to fundamental rights. The possibility for a complaint decreases not only the government's possibility to abuse the state of exception to restrict fundamental rights but also compensates problems related to already implemented restrictions. It is possible, for example, that the realised restrictions are deemed unjustifiable from the perspective of certain groups of people, such as children or disabled people. In Finland, COVID-19 restrictions have also been widely complained about by individual citizens (Chancellor of Justice, 2020, 2021; Parliamentary Ombudsman of Finland, 2021).[4]

DISCUSSION: THE RULE OF LAW DURING AND AFTER COVID-19

In Finland, the trust in authorities, such as courts, the police and the defence forces, has traditionally been high, but Finns also trust greatly their political institutions, such as the parliament, government and president (see e.g. OECD, 2021). Hence, it is not surprising that studies have shown that citizens have mainly trusted political institutions, such as the government, also during the state of exception launched as a result of COVID-19 (Jallinoja & Väliverronen, 2021).

It is obvious that Finland's strength as a *Rechtsstaat* in normal times is based on, one hand, the fact that social institutions have become worth the trust, and, on the other hand, on the fact that institutions indeed are trusted. Therefore, it is paradoxical that during a moderate state of exception, trust can also become a problem: the government is trusted, although on the basis of the state of exception, it violates or restricts constitutionally guaranteed equality of entrepreneurs (Section 6 of the Finnish Constitution), freedom of movement (Section 9), freedom of assembly and freedom of association (Section 13), protection of property (Section 15), educational rights (Section 16), the right to work and the freedom to engage in commercial activity (Section 18), protection under the law (Section 21) and even the most central right of democracy, electoral and participatory rights (Section 14), as we illustrated in the previous section.

In practice, the government has on the basis of the state of exception restricted most of the relative fundamental rights safeguarded in the Finnish Constitution. Some of the restrictions have concerned key democratic rights, such as electoral and participatory rights. It is telling that trust was maintained even when the government considered that delaying elections is necessary in a democratic society. This leads us to ask, whether trust can be too high, as philosopher Tuomas Nevanlinna (2020) has asked when pondering why the limitations to individual rights during the Finnish state of exception have been so easily accepted. In other words, the question is whether trust can be so high that it starts to weaken the resilience of the rule of law.

According to Nevanlinna, the extent of Finns' trust can be explained with functional democracy: unlike in dictatorships, in democracies, the government can be criticised without fear of revenge. Hence, the government can be trusted, at depth, even when people (or the opposition) disagree on the measures. The trust, however, can result in the government starting to restrict, in a state of exception, fundamental rights more than is actually necessary (Nevanlinna, 2020). For example, there has been a public debate in Finland on the government imposing more extensive restrictions on fundamental rights than recommended by experts or health authorities (e.g. Mutanen & Merimaa, 2022). One of the dangers of states of exception is that the government starts to consider itself almighty.

It is clear that in a democracy, government trust does not need to be absolute, but it is enough that the government can have confidence in the support of the majority. Hence, criticism towards the government in a state of exception is not an insurmountable problem for the government, as long as the majority trusts that the restrictions to fundamental rights in a state of exception are justified.

The main argument of the Finnish government during COVID-19 has, in practice, been that individual rights have had to be compromised in order to safeguard people's life and health (e.g. Finnish Government, 2021a). This argument has a strong intuitive power, which is why it easily receives support.

People's trust towards the government benefits the society, which is why there is no need to criticise the atmosphere of trust. In a democratic *Rechtsstaat*, however, one needs to have a sufficiently cautious approach to the government enjoying the trust of the majority in a state of exception. There is a risk that the state ends up in a tyranny of the majority, that is, in a situation that the democratic *Rechtsstaat* has been created to tackle. What we mean is that in a democratic *Rechtsstaat*, individual rights are fully valid precisely in order to prevent the majority from oppressing the minority, as happened in Europe during the Second World War (e.g. Hyttinen, 2019, p. 97). In normal times, individual rights are well realised in Finland, but in a state of exception, the trust towards the government leaves room for the predominance of the majority: even severe restrictions to fundamental rights are acceptable as long as they do not concern the majority.

When analysing the situation from the Finnish perspective, it can be observed that the restrictions during a state of exception have actually mainly been directed at certain people, groups or professions. It is easier to prevent people working in culture from doing their job (by closing, for example, art exhibitions and concert halls), because it has no immediate effects on the basic functions of the society. It is easier to restrict the movement of older people than to order the entire nation to stay home. It is easier to close the schools as long as adults can continue to work. The risk of a restrained state of exception is precisely that it does not radically impact the everyday life of the majority, but their life continues to a large extent as in normal times. This creates a circle in which a government making selected restrictions maintains its trust in the eyes of the majority, and the trust capital enables ever more restrictions. The balance is kept as long as the everyday life of the majority is not too strongly affected.

It has to be emphasised that even though they are problematic, the restrictions imposed in Finland can be defended with the argumentation familiar to us from the philosophy of the state of exception: it has been necessary to compromise the rights of certain individuals in order to safeguard other people's rights. This argument, however, hides the fact that the imposed restrictions to fundamental rights have actually concerned specifically part of the people.

This should not lead to the conclusion that in Finland, the state of exception would have been exploited (in terms of power) in order to grasp unjustified power on the basis of the pandemic, as seems to have happened in some other countries (on the case of Hungary, see e.g. Győry & Weinberg, 2020).[5] Rather, the question has been of the operational logic of the COVID-19 pandemic, which has forced the government to make choices whereby no solution is better than another. On one hand, it has been necessary to in some way restrict people's movement and mutual interaction, as otherwise the virus could have spread uncontrollably in a situation where the society was not yet ready for an increasing virus load. On the other hand, the government has had to safeguard that the necessary functions of the society are not paralysed, which in itself could lead to a social chaos.

At the same time, it has been necessary to impose restrictions and refrain from imposing them. The situation has resembled a moral dilemma, that is, a situation in which one solution is no better than another. In this kind of a situation, the government has no other option but to choose, decide and bear the political and legal responsibility for the restrictive measures (on the theoretical problems in decision-making during a state of exception, see Lagerspetz, 2002, pp. 46–51).

In a functioning democracy, the dangerousness of a state of exception is relativised by the fact that it does not continue forever. It is ended as soon as the government deems it justified, which is necessary to maintain the trust of the government. The most serious threat to a democratic *Rechtstaat* are not the states of exception during COVID-19 but – paradoxically – that a government that needs trust cannot continue the state of exception forever or always declare a new state of exception. Hence, the government has an interest in including the measures used during a state of exception into normal legislation. New states of exception are not needed, because rights can be restricted on the basis of normal legislation. In Finland, changes have been made, for example, in the Communicable Diseases Act (L1227/2016) in order not to make recourse to the Emergency Powers Act in future pandemics. A comprehensive reform of the Communicable Diseases Act is also being prepared, the actual purpose of which is to include regulation that was previously considered to be emergency legislation into normal legislation.

The situation resembles Agamben's argument that states of exception are no longer exceptions, but the emergency legislation has become the rule (Agamben, 2020). The question can deal with the normalisation of states of exception but also with the situation we described earlier, that is, that restrictions to fundamental rights that were previously possible only during a state of exception become possible in normal legislation. In a manner, this normalisation of exceptional measures can also be considered continuation of the state of exception without a formal state of exception.

The normalisation of the legislation related to a state of exception seems to have been assumed as the rule in the COVID-19 Finland, and this trajectory cannot be considered only a positive matter. First of all, when the state of exception is over and COVID-19 has become a mainly theoretical threat, what remains is the normal legislation that would not have been probably considered to comply with democracy and rule of law before COVID-19. Hence, when the following virus (or other threat) emerges, the fundamental rights of individuals can be restricted more easily than before even without a state of exception, which, as a rule, cannot be considered satisfactory in a democratic *Rechtsstaat*. Second, when the measures related to the state of exception are included in normal legislation, power previously part of the state of exception is transferred to public authorities. Even though removing emergency powers from the government may contribute to safeguarding the rule of law, it is not satisfactory that even significant restrictions to fundamental rights can be made by public authorities in the future – without political responsibility.

It has already been visible in Finland that the power to restrict fundamental rights (during COVID-19) has increasingly moved from the government to public authorities. This may constitute a slippery slope, because while the authorities receive more emergency powers, the government wants to assume more powers that go beyond the previous emergency powers. An example of this is a statement of the Finnish Prime Minister Marin that the government would need to be able to do more than normal legislation enables for public authorities.[6]

During COVID-19, in our view, the greatest risk to the rule of law was not the Emergency Powers Act, but the most serious risk lies in the actions that have been or will be realised in the aftermath of the state of exception.

The risk in normalising the state of exception as part of normal legislation should not be undermined, because it does not only concern preparation for future crises. Equally, the question relates to the fact that restrictions to fundamental rights enacted in normal legislation can be used even in smaller crises than states of exception. One can, for example, ponder if fundamental rights are restricted in the future on the basis of a more serious influenza virus, if (and when) the post-COVID legislative amendments enable it. At least, it would seem a more unlikely scenario that on the basis of the influenza virus, a state of exception would be declared, which pre-COVID, would have been the only option to restrict some fundamental rights during an epidemic. There is also a risk that the threshold for declaring a state of exception becomes lower during other types of crises. The problem does not only concern Finland, but as the Finnish example shows, there are always risks included in emergency powers even in countries with the highest rule of law index (see also e.g. De Angelis & De Oliveira, 2021; Kipfer & Mohamud, 2021).

CONCLUSION

The traditional idea of a *Rechtsstaat* can be traced back to the following maxim: use of power in a society cannot be erased and therefore it needs to be controlled (Lagerspetz 2002, p. 58). In addition, the current starting point in the era of democratic *Rechtsstaat* is that fundamental rights set absolute limits to the use of power. In practice, this means that legislation ignoring fundamental rights or application of the law without considering fundamental rights is not acceptable use of power (Ferrajoli, 2007, p. 323).

Typically, the question on the right of a *Rechtsstaat* to compromise its own key values has related to situations where the state has been faced by a military or other violent crisis. Historically, this has also impacted the discussion in philosophy, political science and jurisprudence, whereby the state of exception has been mainly addressed as a radical state of exception. Hence, it needs to be emphasised that in the context of the COVID-19 pandemic and the crisis situation spurred by it has dealt with a more restrained state of exception than in the wartime states of exception in the 20th century. Yet, the fundamental question is the same: how much can a democratic *Rechtsstaat* compromise its own premises without losing its status as a *Rechtsstaat*?[7]

The question is difficult to answer due to the fact that the problems of the state of exception cannot be abolished with norms (Lagerspetz, 2002, p. 58), even though there might be willingness to do so in a *Rechtsstaat*. The difficulty relates to the fact that the attempt to regulate a normative framework to control the power in a state of exception requires an assumption of a typical case of a state of exception, that is, 'a normal state of exception', for which the norms have been stipulated (as also argued by Lagerspetz, 2002, p. 58). States of exception would not, however, constitute genuine states of exception if they never included any surprising and unprecedented threat.

Threats that the Finnish democratic *Rechtsstaat* will face in the future may be very different from what we can imagine at the moment. For example, the Emergency Powers Act that entered into force in 2012 has proved to be problematic already during COVID-19, which demonstrates that it is difficult to prepare to future threats beforehand. Therefore, Finland has again launched a comprehensive reform of the Emergency Powers Act, the aim of which is to more specifically and more comprehensively determine how the government may use its power during different states of exception (Finnish Ministry of Justice, 2021). Nothing guarantees, however, that the possible new Emergency Powers Act would function in future states of exception any better than the current Emergency Powers Act has functioned during the COVID-19 pandemic. Simply put, there are no grounds to expect that neither the future threats will remain within the framework created by the new Emergency Powers Act.

In our chapter, we have argued that the states of exception declared during the coronavirus pandemic have not as such meant erosion of the rule of law in Finland. Individual fundamental rights have been restricted, but the states of exception have been ended as soon as possible. In this sense, the Finnish democratic *Rechtsstaat* has been strong enough to endure the states of exception caused by COVID-19.

Instead, we have criticised two developments caused by COVID-19, which have not been unproblematic from the perspective of the rule of law. On one hand, the attempt to minimise the state of exception has led to the fact that previous emergency powers have been included in normal legislation. This has meant not only increase in the power of public authorities but also a debate on the need to extend the possibility of the government to use power in a state of exception. This creates a circle where the increasing power of public authorities creates a need to increase the power of the politicians. Currently, the power of the politicians (i.e. the government) during a state of exception is sought to be enlarged by stipulating a new Emergency Powers Act.

Hence, the per se good intentions of the Finnish government (evading the declaration of a state of exception) have led to a situation where fundamental rights can in the future be more easily restricted both with normal legislation as well as in possible new states of exception. This development will challenge the resilience of the Finnish democratic *Rechtsstaat* in a new manner.

NOTES

1. The issue is reflected in Professor Emeritus (Constitutional Law) Antero Jyränki's statement from the 1980s. According to Jyränki (1989), in legislation, stating that something is contrary to the constitution 'is thus an exception, which has to have weighty grounds' (p. 294). Jyränki's perspective has been interpreted to refer to the fact that in the 1980s, the constitutional control of legislation was considered unnecessary, and even problematic from the perspective of democracy in Finland (Viljanen, 2001, p. 354). This meant, among other issues, that in legislation and legal praxis, constitutional assessment and argumentation was considered unnecessary, even dangerous.

2. The state of exception is regulated by the Constitution (Act 731/1999, Section 23) and by the Emergency Powers Act (Act 1551/2011). According to the main rule of Section 6(1) of the Emergency Powers Act, cooperation is required from the government and the President, which means that in practice both have to agree that a state of exception prevails in the country. After this, the government has the right to side-line legislation of normal times and provide decrees concerning the state of exception. The provision of decrees does not involve the president's contribution, but the government alone has the power to issue decrees. However, declaring a state of exception does not yield the government an unlimited mandate, but rather a limited one. In practice, the limited mandate is based on the Constitution, Section 23 of which provides on the safeguarding of basic rights and liberties in situations of emergency. Finland is a model country in how the Constitution can aim at ex ante limiting the power of those holding power also during a state of exception (see Section 23(1) of the Constitution). In addition, the power of the government has been sought to be limited in a way that decrees provided during a state of exception (restrictions to fundamental rights) have to be without delay assessed by the Parliament (Constitution, Section 23(2)), thus ultimately the Parliament may decide on the acceptability of the restrictions. In principle, Finland has a modern legislation for a state of exception (the Constitution was amended in 2012 and the Emergency Powers Act was also completely renewed in 2012). Modern legislation does not, however, abolish theoretical and practical problems related to the state of exception. For example, Finland has typically a majority government, which means that the government has good chances – also in a state of exception – to receive parliamentary support for its actions.

3. They did not use the power to decide the competent authority in unclear cases.

4. 2021 Annual Report of the Parliamentary Ombudsman (pp. 163–167) describes the impact of COVID-19 on the workload of the Office of the Parliamentary Ombudsman. Annual Report 2020 of the Chancellor of Justice of the Government and the statistics of the Chancellor of Justice of the Government from 2021 (especially p. 11) reflect the workload caused by COVID-19 for the Chancellor of Justice.

5. It is, of course, possible that even during a state of exception, decisions are guided by political aims such as assessing how much the decided restrictions impact the support for the government parties.

6. Televised interview on Ykkösaamu, YLE 13 March 2021.

7. While finalising the chapter, also the traditional question of a war-time state of exception and its limits has again become concrete in Europe after the Russian invasion of Ukraine in February 2022. In addition to Ukraine, also several countries close to Ukraine (Hungary, Lithuania and Moldova) have declared on the basis of the war a state of exception, which forces us to consider concretely the risks related to the rule of law that may be involved in the abuse of the state of exception. For example, there have been accusations with regard to Hungary that the state of exception declared under the cover of the war in Ukraine has been used to centralise power to the Prime Minister and his party (e.g. Gijs, 2022).

REFERENCES

Agamben, G. (2005). *State of exception.* University of Chicago Press.
Agamben, G. (2020, July 30). *Stato di eccezione e stato di emergenza.* Quodlibet. https://www.quodlibet.it/giorgio-agamben-stato-di-eccezione-e-stato-di-emergenza.
Benjamin, W. (2003). On the concept of history. In H. Eiland & M. W. Jennings (Eds.), *Selected writings Vol. 4: 1938–1940* (pp. 389–400). Harvard University Press.
Blomberg, J. (2011). *Vakauden kaipuu – Kylmän sodan loppu ja Suomi.* WSOY.
Chancellor of Justice. (2020). *Valtioneuvoston oikeuskanslerin kertomus vuodelta 2020.* https://oikeuskansleri.fi/documents/1428954/98543495/oikeuskanslerin_kertomus_2020.pdf/aec869aa-9021-a8d4-c854-daa3f1c5dffb/oikeuskanslerin_kertomus_2020.pdf?t=1637062178951
Chancellor of Justice. (2021). *Valtioneuvoston oikeuskanslerin tilastot vuodelta 2021.* https://oikeuskansleri.fi/documents/1428954/99368527/OKV_Tilastot_2021.pdf/49748b04-1f22-6755-be04-e28e7ed708ba/OKV_Tilastot_2021.pdf?t=1646219685208

Cornell, A. J., & Salminen, J. (2018). Emergency laws in comparative constitutional law – The case of Sweden and Finland. *German Law Journal, 19*(2), 219–250. https://doi.org/10.1017/s2071832200022677

De Angelis, G., & De Oliveira, E. (2021). COVID-19 and the "state of exception": Assessing institutional resilience in consolidated democracies – A comparative analysis of Italy and Portugal. *Democratization, 28*(8), 1602–1621. https://doi.org/10.1080/13510347.2021.1949296

Edgell, A. B., Lachapelle, J., Lührmann, A., & Maerz, S. F. (2021). Pandemic backsliding: Violations of democratic standards during COVID-19. *Social Science and Medicine, 285*(114244), 1–10. https://doi.org/10.1016/j.socscimed.2021.114244

Ferrajoli, L. (2007). The past and the future of the rule of law. In P. Costa & D. Zolo (Eds.), *The rule of law history, theory and criticism* (pp. 323–352). Springer.

Finnish Government. (2020a). *Hallituksen esitys eduskunnalle laiksi majoitus- ja ravitsemistoiminnasta annetun lain väliaikaisesta muuttamisesta, HE 25/2020 vp*.

Finnish Government. (2020b). *Valtioneuvoston asetus kunnan oikeudesta poiketa terveydenhuollon kiireettömän hoidon määräaikojen noudattamisesta ja sosiaalihuollon palvelutarpeen arvioinneista, 127/2020 (2020)*.

Finnish Government. (2020c). *Valtioneuvoston asetus väliaikaisista poikkeuksista sovellettaessa eräitä vuosilomalain, työaikalain ja työsopimuslain säännöksiä, 128/2020 (2020)*.

Finnish Government. (2020d). *Valtioneuvoston asetus valmiuslain 118 §:ssä säädettyjen toimivaltuuksien käyttöönotosta annetun valtioneuvoston asetuksen ja liikkumisen tilapäisistä rajoituksista väestön suojaamiseksi annetun valtioneuvoston asetuksen kumoamisesta, 217/2020 (2020)*.

Finnish Government. (2020e). *Valtioneuvoston asetus valmiuslain 86, 88, 93–95 ja 109 §:ssä säädettyjen toimivaltuuksien käyttöönotosta, 125/2020 (2020)*.

Finnish Government. (2020f). *Valtioneuvoston asetus valmiuslain 87 §:ssä säädettyjen toimivaltuuksien käyttöönotosta välittömästi, 124/2020 (2020)*.

Finnish Government. (2020g). *Valtioneuvoston asetus varhaiskasvatuksen sekä opetuksen ja koulutuksen järjestämisvelvollisuutta koskevista väliaikaisista rajoituksista, 126/2020 (2020)*.

Finnish Government. (2021a). *Government proposal HE 39/2021 vp*.

Finnish Government. (2021b). *Government proposal HE 33/2021 vp*.

Finnish Ministry of Justice. (2021, December 8). *Valmiuslain uudistaminen käynnistyy*. https://valtioneuvosto.fi/-//1410853/valmiuslain-uudistaminen-kaynnistyy

Finnish Parliament Constitutional Committee. (2021). *Perustuslakivaliokunnan lausunto PeVL 12/2021 vp - HE 39/2021 vp*.

Gijs, C. (2022, May 25). *Orbán declares state of emergency due to war in Ukraine*. Politico. https://www.politico.eu/article/viktor-orban-state-emergency-ukraine-war/

Győry, C., & Weinberg, N. (2020). Emergency powers in a hybrid regime: The case of Hungary. *The Theory and Practice of Legislation, 8*(3), 329–353. https://doi.org/10.1080/20508840.2020.1838755

Hallberg, P. (2004). *The rule of law*. Edita.

Heinikoski, S., & Hyttinen, T. (2022). The impact of COVID-19 on the free movement regime in the North. Analysis of border closures in Denmark, Finland, Norway and Sweden. *Nordic Journal of International Law, 2022*(91), 80–100.

Heinonen, T., & Lavapuro, J. (2012). Suomen oikeuden eurooppalaistuminen ja valtiosääntöistyminen 1990–2012. In T. Heinonen & J. Lavapuro (Eds.), *Oikeuskulttuurin Eurooppalaistuminen. Ihmisoikeuksien murroksesta kansainväliseen vuorovaikutukseen* (pp. 7–28). Suomalainen Lakimiesyhdistys.

Hemmilä, I. (2021, March 8). Ravintoloiden sulku voimaan päivän aiottua myöhemmin — suurin osa Suomen maakunnista rajoituksen piirissä. *Turun Sanomat*. https://www.ts.fi/uutiset/5247597

Heupel, M., Koenig-Archibugi, M., Kreuder-Sonnen, C., Patberg, M., Séville, A., Steffek, J., & White, J. (2021). Emergency politics after globalization. *International Studies Review, 23*(4), 1959–1987. https://doi.org/10.1093/isr/viab021

Hyttinen, T. (2015). *Syytön tai syyllinen. Tutkimus syyllisyyskysymyksen ratkaisemisesta*. Suomalainen Lakimiesyhdistys.

Hyttinen, T. (2019). Vihapuhe ja oikeuksien väärinkäytön kielto. In D. Frände, D. Helenius, H. Korkka, R. Lahti, T. Lappi-Seppälä, & S. Melander (Eds.), *Juhlajulkaisu Kimmo Nuotio 1959 – 18/4 – 2019* (pp. 89–111). University of Helsinki.

Jallinoja, P., & Väliverronen, E. (2021). Suomalaisten luottamus instituutioihin ja asiantuntijoihin COVID19-pandemiassa. *Media & Viestintä, 44*(1), 1–24. https://doi.org/10.23983/mv.107298

Jyränki, A. (1989). *Lakien laki: perustuslaki ja sen sitovuus eurooppalaisessa ja pohjoisamerikkalaisessa oikeusajattelussa suurten vallankumousten kaudelta toiseen maailmansotaan*. Lakimiesliiton kustannus.

Kipfer, S., & Mohamud, J. (2021). The pandemic as political emergency. *Studies in Political Economy, 102*(3), 268–288. https://doi.org/10.1080/07078552.2021.2000212

Kortteinen, J. (1996). Sananvapaus ihmisoikeutena. In K. Nordenstreng (Ed.), *Sananvapaus* (pp. 32–88). WSOY.

Lagerspetz, E. (2002). Oikeusvaltion itsepuolustus ja tuho. In A. Aarnio & T. Uusitupa (Eds.), *Oikeusvaltio* (pp. 39–60). Kauppakaari.

Länsineva, P. (2011). Perusoikeusliike. In T. Hyttinen & K. Weckström (Eds.), *Turun yliopiston oikeustieteellinen tiedekunta 50 vuotta* (pp. 339–355). Faculty of Law of the University of Turku.

MacIntyre, A. (1982). *After virtue: A study in moral theory*. Duckworth.

Mutanen, A., & Merimaa, J. (2022, May 23). Kuka kuiski Kiurun korvaan? *Helsingin Sanomat*. https://www.hs.fi/politiikka/art-2000008808227.html

Nevanlinna, T. (2020, March 28). Poikkeustilan julistaminen on äärimmäistä vallankäyttöä, mutta ratkaiseva hetki koittaa, kun se lakkautetaan. YLE. https://yle.fi/aihe/artikkeli/2020/03/28/tuomas-nevanlinna-poikkeustilan-julistaminen-on-aarimmaista-vallankayttoa-mutta

Nuotio, K. (2020). Oikeuslähdeoppia suomalaiseen tapaan. *Lakimies, 118*(7–8), 1236–1249.

OECD. (2021). *Drivers of trust in public institutions in Finland. Building trust in public institutions*. OECD Publishing. https://doi.org/10.1787/52600c9e-en

Parliamentary Ombudsman of Finland. (2021). *Eduskunnan oikeusasiamiehen kertomus vuodelta 2021*. https://www.oikeusasiamies.fi/documents/20184/42383/kertomus2021.pdf/abfe8917-fe87-8630-1100-2527a905a0e8?t=1655809653034

Prime Minister's Office Finland. (2020a). *Muistio: Valtioneuvoston asetus valmiuslain 86, 88, 93-95 ja 109 §:ssä säädettyjen toimivaltuuksien käyttöönotosta*. https://valtioneuvosto.fi/delegate/file/69420

Prime Minister's Office Finland. (2020b, March 16). *Poikkeusolojen toteaminen 16.3.2020*. https://valtioneuvosto.fi/paatokset/paatos?decisionId=0900908f8068ec10

Prime Minister's Office Finland. (2020c, March 25). *Muistio: Valtioneuvoston asetus valmiuslain 118 §:ssä säädettyjen toimivaltuuksien käyttöönotosta*. https://valtioneuvosto.fi/delegate/file/69477

Prime Minister's Office Finland. (2020d, June 15). *Muistio: Valmiuslaissa säädettyjen toimivaltuuksien käytön ja valmiuslain mukaisten poikkeusolojen päättyminen*. https://valtioneuvosto.fi/delegate/file/73412

Prime Minister's Office Finland. (2021a, March 1). *Poikkeusolojen toteaminen 1.3.2021*. https://valtioneuvosto.fi/paatokset/paatos?decisionId=0900908f80711e0a

Prime Minister's Office Finland. (2021b, April 27). *Muistio: Valmiuslaissa säädettyjen toimivaltuuksien käytön ja valmiuslain mukaisten poikkeusolojen päättyminen*. https://valtioneuvosto.fi/delegate/file/89206

Puumalainen, M. (2018). *EU:n etusijaperiaate Suomen valtiosääntöoikeudessa*. Suomalainen Lakimiesyhdistys.

Scheppele, K. L. (2004). Law in a time of emergency: states of exception and the temptations of 9/11. *Journal of Constitutional Law, 6*(5), 1001–1083.

Schmitt, K. (2005). *Political theology. Four chapters on the concept of sovereignty* (G. Schwab, Trans.). Chicago University Press.

Taylor, C. (1994). *Multiculturalism: Examining the politics of recognition* (A. Gutmann, Ed.). Princeton University Press.

Tuori, K. (1992). Four models of the Rechtsstaat. In W. Krawietz & G. H. von Wright (Eds.), *Öffentliche oder private Moral? Vom Geltungsgrunde und der Legitimität des Rechts* (pp. 451–464). Duncker & Humblot.

Tuori, K. (2003). Tuomarivaltio – Uhka vai myytti? *Lakimies*, 2003(6), 915–943.

Viljanen, V.-P. (2001). *Perusoikeuksien rajoitusedellytykset*. Talentum.

Walzer, M. (1983). *Spheres of justice: A defense of pluralism and equality*. Martin Robertson.

CHAPTER 5

CONSTITUTIONALISM AND EMERGENCY RULE: COMPARING GERMANY'S AND SPAIN'S RESPONSES TO THE COVID-19 PANDEMIC

José María Rosales

University of Málaga, Spain

ABSTRACT

Regulated differently in modern constitutions, emergency rule is a case of awkward, and dilemmatic, legal fine-tuning of an ambivalent political move that leads the executive of a democratic regime to the verge of the constitutional system. For that reason, as an utmost situation, emergency rule becomes a testing field for the resilience of the constitutional order. It affects its own foundations, the basic rights, and thus the constitutional capability to make possible their fulfilment. It also serves to appraise the workings of democratic regimes and, accordingly, the type of legitimacy derived from their institutional performance. Furthermore, it provides a vantage point to watch the reactions of both their representatives and their publics. Focussed on the COVID-19 pandemic, this chapter compares the cases of Germany and Spain through their legal regulations of emergency rule and their governments' responses. Having rather analogous emergency legislations, from

2020 through 2022, there have been significant differences in their decision-making patterns.

Keywords: Constitutionalism; emergency rule; Germany's emergency laws; Spain's emergency laws; COVID-19 pandemic

Tackling the COVID-19 pandemic, whose first outbreak dates from December 2019, has become an instructive example to survey political responses across countries. Reactions to curb the pandemic, despite being guided by public health goals, are the outcome of political decisions. In this regard, comparisons among democratic regimes are especially meaningful, for under akin conditions, resorting or not to emergency powers makes a great difference (see e.g. Goetz & Martinsen, 2021). It attests in varying degrees not only to each government's accommodation to its constitutional role but also to each country's constitutional and parliamentary cultures.

Emergency rule, governing under emergency conditions, adds a disquieting challenge to normal politics, because drawing on extraordinary measures to be used within a fixed time span, even if a legal option, tests constitutional orders to their limits. In particular, among European democracies, comparisons provide information about the uses, and abuses, of emergency powers, persuasively evincing that their leaders have not been safe from autocratic leanings. And although, in this case, democratic governments have accessed a similar stock of constitutional instruments, as can be inquired through the Venice Commission of the Council of Europe's Observatory on Emergency Situations (Venice Commission, 2022), their responses through the consecutive waves of the pandemic well into 2022 bring to light very different understandings of the functioning of constitutional democracy.

This chapter aims to compare the uses of emergency powers in two constitutional democracies, Germany and Spain. Both share basic constitutional arrangements, and the Spanish constitutional politics over the past century has largely followed the German example. Yet, there has been a remarkable difference as regards the grounds for emergency rule claimed by the government of each country. Their decision-making strategies from 2020 to 2022 have advanced in divergent directions: towards a stronger centralisation in Germany and towards a rising decentralisation in Spain. Such contrast, it is argued as a hypothesis, is not just a result of institutional differences. It is also an outcome of their mismatched constitutional and parliamentary cultures regardless of the many parallels that exist between their emergency laws.

The first section of this chapter presents the rationale for the comparison between the German and the Spanish constitutional orders. The second section selects some representative aspects of German constitutional understandings of emergency rule. The third section focusses on Spain's partly synchronous history of legal adjustments of what turns out to be an ambivalent political move. An account of their contrasting political decisions in response to the COVID-19 pandemic is given in the fourth section. The chapter finally weighs up the constitutional and political effects of this extraordinary recourse.

EMERGENCY POWERS IN GERMANY AND SPAIN: THE COMPARISON IN BRIEF

Regarding the constitutional intricacies of emergency rule, its political uses, and their surrounding debates Germany has gathered, for more than a century, a broad and telling experience (see e.g. Dyzenhaus, 2012). Deeply affected by its overuse during the Weimar Republic through the 1920s and 1930s, and its contentious legal and political effects, the later constitutional recasting of emergency powers from 1949 has unremittingly proceeded against that background. That experience keeps inspiring disputes about the aptness and proportionality of emergency rule, and also remains as a needful reservoir of comparative knowledge outside of Germany.

Because of its exemplary character, in matters of emergency laws the constitutional histories of other democracies, not just from Europe, have looked into the mirror of Germany's. Even though concerning its usages, quite a few transnational comparisons are of interest; out of all cases, a number of very significant parallels and variances are traceable from the 1930s till the present between Germany and Spain. Their contrast provides a distinctive view of how and why similar normative instruments are taken into political practice in rather divergent ways.[1]

To begin with, the 20th-century constitutional history of Spain, through its polity's democratising changes of the 1930s and the 1970s, has found in German constitution-making, and in particular its grounds for emergency powers, a fruitful precedent. Yet, the similarities between their state structure and powers are not many, and their differences shed light on each country's distinct decision-making patterns and governability conditions. For example, there is a lack of correspondence between each country's upper chamber of parliament, being the *Bundesrat*, the representative chamber for Germany's 16 federated states (*Länder*), whereas that function is only having a symbolic role in the Senate for Spain's 17 autonomous communities (*comunidades autónomas*). So, being Spain constitutionally a federal-like state, displaying indeed noticeable differences with federal countries, its governing approach throughout the COVID-19 pandemic has gradually become more decentralised than those of federal Germany's two executives (a new government took office on 8 December 2021).

Conceptualisations of emergency rule in the Weimar Constitution (the Constitution of the German Empire) of 1919 and the Basic Law of 1949 were partially reproduced in Spain's 1931 and 1978 Constitutions. A greater resemblance became discernible through the ordinary laws and decrees enacted in Germany from the 1920s and in Spain during the 1930s; and later on, between the constitutional amendment of 1968 in Germany and the Spanish emergency law of 1981. Their conceptual affinities in emergency legislation are noteworthy, but no parallels exist between political decision-making patterns in each country under emergency conditions beyond the 1930s. Only of late, all round the several waves of the pandemic from 2020 to 2022, Germany's and Spain's governments have shown partly coincident reactions. To a great extent, they resemble those of other democracies, in particular their trial and error paths.

Concerning their political performance there is, however, another noteworthy difference which lies in the role fulfilled under emergency conditions by each parliament, and most notably their lower chambers. Thus whereas Germany's *Bundestag* has kept during the pandemic many of its regular activities going on, Spain's Congress of Deputies has shrunk them, especially the parliamentary oversight of the executive and parliament's legislative production, the latter largely replaced by governmental decrees. A different matter has to do with regional parliaments for the time of the pandemic, as some similarities exist due to their downsized role in front of expanding executives.

Being the German and the Spanish constitutional provisions fairly comparable, their political strategies (and no major change came with the new German government after December 2021) display very different grasps of the uses of emergency rule, backed in each case by parliamentary majorities, and the running under emergency conditions of a constitutional democracy.

HOW EMERGENCY RULE TESTS CONSTITUTIONAL ORDERS: GERMANY'S LESSONS

One of modern constitutionalism's insights was that under normal political circumstances even freely elected governments tend to exceed their own powers (McIlwain, 1947, pp. 123–146). So from the end of the 18th century, the elements of modern democratic thought (from ideas to institutional blueprints, practices, techniques, and procedures) began to be carried out in institution building experiments across Europe and America, it became apparent that the separation of sovereign and government easily faded away at the expense of the sovereign people. Keeping a democratic government in check required further institutional oversights that liberal constitutions have devised ever since; and no less important, it also demanded permanent vigilance from other representative institutions, in particular parliaments, and from citizens alike.

Long after, at the interwar constitutional debates, the controversies around emergency powers were interpreted in a new light. On the one hand, the Weimar experience cast doubts on their convenience and reasonability: the longer their use, the more difficult would become to restore the proper functioning of a constitutional democracy. This is probably the main political lesson whose worth has endured the passage of time till the present. Article 48 section 2 of the Weimar Constitution empowered the Reich president, and article 48 section 4 the *Länder* governments, when 'public security and order' were at risk, to take measures to restore them even at the price of suspending (*außer Kraft setzen*) basic rights. No corresponding empowerment would be granted to the federal president or the governments of federal provinces (*Länder*) by the Austrian Constitution of 1920 (articles 60–68 B-VG) which revised the prerogatives enjoyed by the Austro-Hungarian emperor-king. Conceivably the 1918 and 1919 revolutionary events in Germany played a part in the constitutional project, especially as regards the balance of authority between president and parliament.

While in force, this constitutional authorisation to rule by decree became almost the norm, thus severely disabling parliamentary oversight (on this paradoxical move of parliamentary supremacy, see in comparative perspective e.g. Lindseth, 2004, pp. 1343–1349). Under Friedrich Ebert, the first president on the Weimar Republic, fifteen emergency decrees (*Notverordnungen*) were approved in 1919, eight in 1920, twelve in 1921, and ten in 1922; under Paul von Hindenburg, the second president, one emergency decree was approved in 1925, three in 1930, thirteen in 1931, and three in 1932; then in the transit towards the Third Reich regime, twenty in 1933, and three in 1934 (*Notverordnungen*, 2004). Besides, from 1920 to 1927 seven 'empowering' laws (*Ermächtigungsgesetze*) were approved, mostly to deal with the mounting economic crisis (*Wissenschaftliche Dienste des Deutschen Bundestages*, 2014, pp. 8–11). The last one, completing the neutralisation of the *Reichstag* and inaugurating the National Socialist period, was the Law to remedy the misery of the people and the empire (*Gesetz zur Behebung der Not von Volk und Reich*), approved on 24 March 1933.

On the other hand, this controversial shift in constitutionalism (accelerated through the Weimar years), which in some way rehabilitated the doctrine of reason of state in a democracy, became the object of constitutional debates. In his *Verfassungslehre*, first published in 1928, Carl Schmitt (2003 [1928]), explains the difficulty and the need to keep these presidential powers within the boundaries of the constitutional order (pp. 26–27 and 111–112) assuming Richard Grau's doctrine of constitutional inviolability (*Unantastbarkeit*). That to protect the constitutional order such extraordinary powers could be required was eloquently portrayed as 'the dictatorial power of Reich presidents and of *Länder* governments' (Grau, 1922). The author of the constitutional draft, Hugo Preuß, whose version of article 48 remained fairly unmodified, would argue afterwards the need of article 48 to protect the integrity of the republic convinced that it would not lead to an emergency regime (Preuß, 2008 [1925]).

So risky was it to find a tempered balance, that in practice it turned likelier to bypass the legal requirements of article 48. Ebert's and Hindenburg's performance fell short of the leadership needed. This remark is not a criticism but an evidence of their unlikely roles to halt the downfall of the Republic (Möller, 2008, pp. 11–82). The overuse of emergency powers set off a vicious circle that for practical purposes rendered parliament powerless, although that was not the only cause of its conundrum. Through successive elections, the rising presence of antiparliamentary groups in the *Reichstag* left it oftentimes trapped in legislative gridlocks (Mommsen, 2009, pp. 329–382; see also the *Wikipedia* entry Reichstagswahlen in Deutschland, 2021).

Government's decisive share in the 'disintegration of the political system' over the last years of the Weimar Republic (Kolb & Schumann, 2013, pp. 130–53) happened, infamously, after chancellor Heinrich Brüning formed in March 1930 his government, known as the first presidential cabinet (*Präsidialkabinett*). President Hindenburg accepted his appeal to rule by emergency decrees as the suitable way to face the economic and social upheaval caused by the world financial crisis. The government sidestepped the parliamentary oversight but its decisions, largely unrestrained, were born without enough legitimacy. In a newspaper piece of April 1930, Otto Kirschheimer (2017 [1930a], pp. 202–205) acutely criticised such a strategy on the grounds of the constitutional distortion that it accomplished. Its title was 'Article 48 – The False Way' (*Artikel 48 – der falsche Weg*).

As further spelt out in a journal essay, the same year, the continued pre-eminence of decrees over ordinary laws ended by sanctioning the *normality of the extraordinary* (Kirschheimer, 2017 [1930b], p. 352). Such exceptional empowerment of the Reich president, also overstretching the reach of government action, did reinterpret the notion of democratic sovereignty.

In a much-cited passage from his book *Politische Theologie*, made up of four chapters on the doctrine of sovereignty, Carl Schmitt presents an intricate account of the idea of sovereignty. Schmitt takes it as a border or limit concept (*Grenzbegriff*) because, unlike other political and legal concepts, he argues, its definition cannot be determined relying on a normal case but on a limit case; in other words, because its meaning cannot be grasped from a normal but from a limit situation. 'The sovereign is the one who decides on the condition of exception' (*Souverän ist, wer über den Ausnahmenzustand entscheidet*), so reads the opening sentence of chapter one (Schmitt, 2009 [1922], p. 13), its last phrase usually, and somehow inaccurately, translated as 'state of exception'. Later on Schmitt (2003 [1928], p. 176) in an academic treatise exemplified this condition of exception with article 48 section 2 of the Weimar Constitution.

Sovereignty was for Schmitt a limit concept to the extent that its meaning arose from a limit situation challenging the exercise of political power, to use John Locke's expression. The condition of exception(ality) curiously illustrated this faculty in both autocratic and democratic regimes. However, in the former case to say that the sovereign, namely, the sovereign ruler, decides on the condition of exception(ality) is a tautology, whereas in the latter case, it is mere enunciation, because a president of a democratic republic or its government is not their sovereigns but their representatives, turns problematic. That is how it was in the 1920s and continues a century later.

When *Politische Theologie* was published, Schmitt's ideas represented not only a scholarly contribution to an old inquiry of the history of legal and political thought. They also resounded in the scholarly and public debates around presidential powers in a parliamentary regime. And more specifically, in the related debates about the effects of constitutionalising the idea of popular sovereignty, with the recent memories of the social democratic Revolution of November 1918 in Bavaria and the counter-revolution of the following months (on the 1918–1919 events, see Haffner, 2018 [1979], pp. 122–138). Both the preamble and article 1 of the Weimar Constitution of 1919 declared that sovereignty lay with the German people. Acknowledging, in the preamble, that the German people 'has endowed itself with this Constitution', article 1 further indicated that this was the legitimising source of the state institutions, after establishing that 'the German Empire is a republic'.

Such act of self-determination was meant as the founding moment of the republic, being a major step in the lengthy transformation, the parliamentarisation, of the Reich into a republic started several decades earlier (Weber, 1988 [1917], pp. 258–275), and hence the legitimating signal to constitute a representative system. Article 178 formally established that the Constitution of the German Empire of 1871 was superseded by the new one. In the republic, the sovereign people act through their representatives – a condition that affected consequently the state's highest office, the Reich president, outlining a delicate mechanism of constitutional checks and balances.

As mentioned above, paragraphs 1 and 2 of article 48 listed the exceptional powers that the Reich president, and paragraph 4 added the *Länder* governments in their territories, could assume in emergency situations, yet always subject to the *Reichstag*. Even though the Reich president could dissolve the *Reichstag* (article 25 section 1 WVerf), as a legislative chamber it had the authority to override the extraordinary executive but also legislative capacity, in emergency situations, of the Reich president and of the *Länder* governments (article 48 section 3 WVerf). Both democratically elected representatives could act in emergency situations as sovereign rulers in their respective jurisdictions and this concerned the possibility that adopting extraordinary measures, aimed at restoring 'public security and order', could entail the partial or whole temporary suspension of basic rights (article 48 section 2 in the case of the Reich president, and article 48 section 4 in the case of federated states governments).

The Weimar Constitution was in force until February 1933. Its conceptualisation and wordings of emergency rule were thoroughly revised by the Basic Law of 1949 which introduced a novel understanding of emergency powers. Actually, the Basic Law regulates in a rather guaranteeing spirit the condition of exception(ality). The phrase is not mentioned, but the idea is mostly rendered by the concept of legislative emergency (*Gesetzgebungsnotstand*) in article 81.

There are two main differences between the Weimar Constitution and the Basic Law regarding emergency rule. One is that the Basic Law authorises constraints on basic rights, but not their suspension. This is exemplified by the right to assembly (article 8 GG) or the confidentiality of correspondence (article 10 GG). Article 19 section 1 further clarifies that any basic right can be restricted (*eingeschränkt*), but the enforceable restrictions must be regulated by law, thus strengthening the general scope of such course of action by banning restrictions prompted by single cases. Regarding suspension, article 19 section 2 establishes that '[i]n no case may a basic right be affected in its essential content' (*In keinem Falle darf ein Grundrecht in seinem Wesensgehalt angetastet werden*).

The other relevant difference is that along with those cases, the first version of the Basic Law (May 23, 1949) only contemplated, in article 81, legislating under the emergency circumstances resulting from a chancellor's failed confidence vote before a new chancellor was appointed (article 68 section 1 GG). Interestingly, article 37 section 1, considering the case that a *Land* is not fulfilling its federal duties, enables the federal government, with the authorisation from the *Bundesrat*, 'to adopt the necessary measures', that is, having recourse to 'federal coercion' (*Bundeszwang*), to make it comply with them. Explicit provisions for the emergency rule were introduced by the constitutional amendment of 1968, the so-called Emergency Acts, *Notstandsgesetze*, that was integrated into the constitutional text.

Only then were emergency situations (*Notsituationen*) surveyed extensively throughout the constitutional articles. The new clauses were enforceable in case of defence (*Verteidigungsfall*), as set out in articles 115a–115l; of natural catastrophe, implying the restriction on freedom of movement (article 11 section 2 GG); or when 'the free democratic basic order of the federation or of a *Land*' is at risk (article 91 section 2 GG). Article 80a considers the enforcement of basic rights restrictions in a case of tension (*Spannungsfall*), officially translated as 'state of tension', namely, a public situation of a lesser tensional degree than the case of defence, requiring a two-thirds majority vote in the *Bundestag* (article 80a section 1 GG) which can cancel it (article 80a section 2 GG), even in the case of obligations derived from international treaties (article 80a section 3 GG).

The many clauses of the 1968 constitutional amendment responded to the requirements the Allies demanded of the Federal Republic to retrieve its full sovereignty. Since then no other constitutional amendments in matters of emergency rule have been made. Further provisions for emergencies were regulated by a law enacted in 2000, the Infection Protection Act (*Infektionsschutzgesetz*) which has been amended in 2020 and 2021. In all cases, the constitutional checks were aimed at finding a pragmatic balance between authorising emergency powers and containing within the constitutional order the consequences of this decisionist move. Its spell during the Weimar years pervaded the debates of the legal profession and the public debates relying on the indemonstrable premise that a critical situation required inexorably the advent of emergency powers.

THE CONTENTIOUS RATIONALE OF EMERGENCY POWERS: SPAIN'S EXPERIENCE

In line with the Weimar Constitution, the Spanish Constitution of 1931 acknowledged in article 42 the recourse to emergency rule 'in cases of clear and imminent graveness', parliament authorising government to enact a decree that, 'when so required by the security of the state', can suspend basic rights partially or wholly. A suspension like that could run on for a maximum of 30 days – any extension requiring a parliamentary agreement thereof. Under emergency rule, a law of public order should be in force. Another similitude, not attaining the German presidential competences, has to do with the status of the president of the republic. The president was entitled to summon parliament 'whenever he deems it appropriate' and to dissolve it up to twice during the presidential six-year term (article 81 CE 1931). The president had the capacity to '[o]rdain the urgent measures required by the defence of the integrity or the security of the nation, reporting at once to parliament (*Cortes*)' (article 76 section d CE 1931). Under emergency conditions, the president could issue decrees whose lawfulness would have a provisional character until parliament either decides or legislates on the matters arousing them (article 80 CE 1931).

However, stronger similarities came with ordinary laws regulating emergency powers. The first one, the so-called Law in Defence of the Republic (*Ley de Defensa de la República*), entered into force on 22 October 1931, approved by the constituent parliament (*Cortes Constituyentes*), since the Constitution of the Spanish Second Republic was approved in December 1931. Drawing, to draft it, on the ongoing parliamentary debates about public order but also anticipating a rise of social upheavals, the provisional government gathered the required number of votes to pass it (see e.g. Bjork & Spohr, 2016). The five-article law granted government the faculty to persecute 'acts of aggression against the Republic' (article 1 LDR). What amounted to those acts could be decided, as stated in article 3, in a discretionary way by the minister of the interior (*Ministro de la Gobernación*), who assumed the enforcement of the law (article 4 LDR) in terms close to those of a state of siege, that is, with the capacity to suspend basic rights.

In the parliamentary session where the draft law was debated, held on 20 October, the independent representative Santiago Alba pointed out that 'it is almost a literal copy of the German law' (*DSCCRE*, No. 59, October 20, 1931, p. 1837). Indeed it fairly reproduced the aims and contents of the two German laws for the protection of the Republic (*Gesetz zum Schutze der Republik*), the first one entering into force on 21 July 1922, and the second one on 25 March 1930. In his reply to criticisms about the paranoid and rushed tone of the project, the head of government (*Presidente del Gobierno*), Manuel Azaña, justified: 'Government does not need this law, the Republic does', to add later: 'The Republic is not at risk, but to avoid that the danger rises, this law is needed' (*DSCCRE*, No. 59, October 20, 1931, p. 1842).

A law of public order (*Ley de Orden Público*) replaced it. Enacted on 30 July 1933, it graded emergency rule from 'state of prevention' (articles 20–33 LOP) to 'state of alarm' (articles 34–47 LOP) and 'state of war' (articles 48–61 LOP). To defend public order or 'public peace' (*paz pública*), as defined in articles 1–5, or to re-establish it, basic rights could be suspended in the two latter cases, while under the first one their enjoyment could be only constrained. That way it revised the dubious constitutionality of the previous law, but its ceaseless invocations by successive governments from August 1933 until the outbreak of the Civil War in July 1936 made impossible a normal functioning of the constitutional order (Ballbé, 1983, pp. 359 ff.).

Besides, the law bolstered the surveillance role of civil governors (*gobernadores civiles*), a 19th-century figure following the French model of *préfets*, who bore the political authority delegated by government in each of the country's territorial units, provinces. There was no equivalence in the German laws at that time, and still later its analogue, the *Regierungspräsidenten*, are under the authority of the *Länder* governments, not the federal government. In so doing, it helped deploy nationwide a network of vigilance whose ominous effectiveness was perfected by Franco's dictatorship since 1939.

In adapting emergency powers to a democratic legality, the Spanish Constitution of 1978 freely interpreted national and international precedents. Article 116 of the Constitution acknowledged emergency rule in correspondence with three levels of emergency, classified as 'states of alarm, exception and siege' (*estados de alarma, de excepción y de sitio*). The three degrees of emergency rule were further regulated by an organic law in 1981. Unlike ordinary laws, in Spain, organic laws regulate constitutional matters concerned with the exercise of basic rights. In this case, its guaranteeing spirit resembles that of the Basic Law after the amendment of 1968. Article 1 section 4 of the law establishes that '[t]he declaration of the states of alarm, exception and siege does not interrupt the normal functioning of the state constitutional powers'. According to article 4 section b, government can declare the state of alarm in health crises by a decree, being its deadline of 15 days, only extendable by authorisation of the Congress of Deputies (article 6 LO 4/1981). While the decree remains in force, government 'will be responsible to the Congress of Deputies' for that declaration and the ensuing norms (article 8 LO 4/1981).

The constraints on basic rights allowed in a state of alarm (article 11 LO 4/1981) are far away from the suspensions envisaged under a state of exception (articles 13ff. LO 4/1981), but the crucial difference lies in the scope of parliamentary oversight in each case. So, whereas under state of alarm, government needs the authorisation of the Congress of Deputies to rule by decree (article 6 section 2 LO 4/1981), a declaration of state of exception has to be debated by Congress (article 13 section 3 LO 4/1981) which means that decisions about its agreement and reach require parliamentary deliberation and voting. Furthermore, whereas there is no time limit to extend state of alarm every 15 days, beyond reason and Congress permitting, under state of exception emergency rule can only be lengthened an extra 30 days (article 15 section 3 LO 4/1981).

In all regards, the Organic Law 4/1981, approved a few months after the failed coup d'état of February that year, restrained the chances of an abuse of emergency powers by the executive. And even if not so comprehensive as the German emergency legislation, the Spanish law reached a high regulatory level. Later on, in terms of constitutional provisions, it came close not just to Germany, but also to Greece, Hungary, Poland, or Portugal (see Khakee, 2009, pp. 9–17). Comparative experience shows that the risk of turning a restriction of basic rights into their suspension seems inescapable. The only reasonable treatment hints that more determining than the thoroughness of the legal regulation of emergency rule is the functioning of the state powers while this is in force and, among them, a government's performance of its extraordinary powers.

WHY EMERGENCY RULE?
A COMPARATIVE GLOSS

A 1995 report prepared for the European Commission for Democracy through Law (the Venice Commission of the Council of Europe), based on comparative data from 32 countries, concluded that 'there is always a potential for the abuse of state power, and experience has shown that the most serious violations of human rights tend to occur in emergency situations' (Özbudun & Turhan, 1995). Acknowledging the shortcomings of constitutionalism under emergency rule, the report recommended that constitutions delimit the margin of manoeuvre that governments attain upon declaring emergency rule.

As is well known, on 30 January 2020, the World Health Organization (WHO) declared a 'public health emergency of international concern'. Notifications from the European Centre for Disease Prevention and Control to European Union (EU) governments began in early January (see e.g. Reusken et al., 2020). All of them were advices to adopt preventive measures assuming, as shown by a WHO-commissioned report, that 'a global coordinated effort is needed to enhance preparedness in other [than China] regions of the world that may need additional support for that' (World Health Organization, 2020).

Most governments, and their public health advisers, expected the COVID-19 impact would match that of previous pandemics and so be curbed like in the past. In Europe, they reacted belatedly. The national health systems have very dissimilar capacities, going from the robust Nordic welfare state institutions to the far less equipped health infrastructures from Eastern Europe. For any observer what made the difference over the first wave, roughly through the first half of 2020, was not so much their safety nets, as the governments' reactions. That helps to understand, for example, the successful case of Romania, unmatched by countries such as Denmark, Finland, or Norway. Yet, the next waves have disproved a prolonged efficacy of the initial responses. By demanding adaptative strategies, the shifting challenges of the pandemic have left clear another factor, namely, the comparative advantage of cooperative styles of ruling.

During the spring of 2020, many governments declared emergency rule. Germany was an exception (see e.g. COVID-19 Civic Freedom Tracker, 2022). To face a pandemic with an ordinary law might seem a reaction too conservative. The German government justified the validity of the 2000 Law for the prevention and control of infectious diseases in humans, known by its short name, Infection Protection Act (*Infektionsschutzgesetz*) which was amended on 27 March 2020. Further, it opted for intensifying the coordination between the federal and the 16 *Länder* governments in public health and security affairs (*Wissenschaftliche Dienste des Deutschen Bundestages*, 2020). Months later and after mounting disagreements between the minister presidents over chancellor Merkel's performance, new amendments to the law, approved on 21 April 2021 (*Deutscher Bundestag*, 2021), were aimed at better harmonising the lifting of mobility restrictions and the triggering of federal emergency brakes (*Bundesnotbremse*) depending on the evolution of infection rates (Steffen, 2021). This has been the only national lockdown. Drawn on paragraph 5 of the Infection Protection Act, it lasted until the end of June 2021. Previous and later ones have been enacted by single federated states.

After declaring state of alarm on 14 March 2020 (Royal Decree 463/2020, of March 14), the Spanish government assumed a unified command which looked in principle a rational choice, though this happened in a much decentralised country where health competencies had been on average since more than three decades transferred to its 17 autonomous communities. By doing so, government saw itself unexpectedly taking on the role of a sovereign. Under emergency rule, this opened a path of legislative activism. Browsing the *Official Bulletin of the State* gives a fair idea[2]: over the first month under state of alarm, government issued 11 royal decrees, 59 orders developing those decrees, and some 22 resolutions further regulating specific aspects of the many legal changes enacted. They covered all areas directly hit by the pandemic, but a closer look revealed that aspects from ordinary laws not related to the public health crisis were also affected. Chances to revoke those legal amendments (e.g. in the public pensions schemes) would presumably depend on Constitutional Court's rulings expected for the following years. A similar pattern continued steadily from the second month onwards.

This overarching legislative production prompted a series of accompanying normative changes in the regional administrations. That was a necessary step to keep the internal consistency between national and regional legislation, given the network structure of the constitutional order, formed by the Spanish Constitution and the Constitutions of the autonomous communities. However, this centripetal process typical of a multilayered system of norms was immediately offset by its centrifugal turn. And so, in parallel, it sparked a manifold legislative activism in the regional governments, most of the time proceeding with diminished parliamentary oversight. That definitely contributed to heightening their many regulatory differences in health care, education, public administration, and taxes. Along with government, their normative zeal advanced at a pace that soon began to ravel Spain's already complex regulatory landscape.

Under state of alarm, parliamentary activity plummeted and the open-government internet portal was switched off. After 99 days of national lockdown a devolution of those competences began, then trying out an experimental coordination between government and regions in the so-called Scaling down plan (*Plan de desescalada*) released on 28 April (*Presidencia del Gobierno, Head of Government's Office*, 2020). The meetings of the Federation-*Länder* conference during the first wave had, seemingly, a replica in the Spanish case. They were less in number but with a streamlined distribution of competences set up by the Basic Law and the Infection Protection Act (*Wissenschaftliche Dienste des Deutschen Bundestages*, 2021); they continued a long-established collaborative practice, full of internal debate indeed. In contrast, as stated in a response of 18 September 2020, to a series of parliamentary queries submitted in early July, although the Spanish ministry of health had for the previous six months convened the Interterritorial Council of the National Health System (*Consejo Interterritorial del Sistema Nacional de Salud*) more than 40 times, and 15 conferences of regional premiers were held (*Respuesta del Gobierno*, 2020), the coordination was focussed on technical aspects of public health.

Unlike in Germany, the political cooperation produced meagre outcomes. Journalist Victoria Prego (2020) described government's attitude as a disclaimer of responsibility. For example, it did not accept the demands by the opposition in parliament and by many regional premiers to use, or to update, the Organic Law 3/1986, of special measures in matters of public health, or the General Law of Health 14/1986. Only at the end of March 2021 was approved the Law 2/2021 of urgent measures of prevention, containment, and coordination to face the health crisis caused by COVID-19.

However, it did not solve the coordination puzzles, as government handed over the high court of each community (*Tribunales Superiores de Justicia*) the duty to inspect the legality of measures applied by regional governments – a government decision later on declared unconstitutional (see Constitutional Court CI. 6283-2020, June 2, 2022). In the last instance, this meant that the Supreme Court (*Tribunal Supremo*) had to decide for each autonomous community the validity of restrictions imposed on basic rights. The post-lockdown was a time of unease about what measures would come next. The opposition had its own share of responsibility for the stalemate created (Cacho, 2020) and the Spanish society gave proof of its civic intelligence (Varela, 2020), though it was government that had the real capacity to seize the political initiative.

At that time it became apparent that new waves of the pandemic would have a more devastating impact on public health, and the economy. An article by an economics professor in the *Neue Zürcher Zeitung* on 10 October cast serious doubt on the country's capacity to efficiently manage the Next Generation funds (Sell, 2020), aimed to boost the recovery of the EU's economies from 2021 to 2023

(European Commission, 2021). Four days later, a chronicle in the *Frankfurter Allgemeine Zeitung* bore an eloquent title, 'Spain Has Lost the Controls' (Rössler, 2020), roughly in the same line as another article in *The Economist* (2020) with the title 'Spain's Poisonous Politics Have Worsened the Pandemic and the Economy'.

On 25 October 2020, emergency rule was again declared (Royal Decree 926/2020, of October 25), yet it was further extended since 9 November for a period of six months (Royal Decree 956/2020, of November 3). Even though restrictions on basic rights would be milder, it received parliamentary approval (Resolution of October 29, 2020, of the Congress of Deputies). In the months that followed the debate over the need and proportionality of such measure broadened and made clear that partial lockdowns could be regulated differently (see Cebada Romero & Domínguez Redondo, 2021), the state of alarm unfolding itself as a powerful protection not for the population but for the executive.

On 14 July, the Constitutional Court (*Tribunal Constitucional*) made public its Ruling 148/2021 declaring unconstitutional several clauses of Royal Decree 463/2020, of March 14, by which the first state of alarm was established; in particular, a number of restrictions on basic rights were declared null because of state of alarm's inadequacy for such purpose (sections 1, 3, and 5 of article 7 of the decree; see e.g. Presno Linera & García Majado, 2021). A few months later, the Court announced its Ruling 183/2021, of October 27. With similar arguments, it also established the partial unconstitutionality of Royal Decree 926/2020, of October 25, declaring the second state of alarm, and of Royal Decree 956/2020, of November 3, that prolonged it.

What especially draws attention in the Court's latter ruling is how it underlines the unconstitutionality not just of government's decision, but also of parliament's consent to extend emergency rule for six months bypassing its own debating and authorisation procedures in emergency situations. Number 8 of its juridical grounds (*fundamentos jurídicos*) is a reminder of the nullity of their interpretations of both the Spanish Constitution and the 1981 emergency law (Constitutional Court, Ruling 183/2021, published in the *Official Bulletin of the State* of November 25, pp. 145308–145323; see an early warning by emeritus judge of the Court Manuel Aragón, 2020).

The contrast with the German case is instructive. In a decision adopted on 19 November 2021, the Federal Constitutional Court (*Bundesverfassungsgericht*) established that the measures taken during the sole national lockdown enacted, in force from 23 April till 30 June 2021, were constitutional (*verfassungsgemäß*). They met the requirements of both formal and material constitutionality (*Verfassungsmäßigkeit*), the former regarding the effective approval of the decision, and the latter regarding the ensuing protection of basic rights, and lastly, they were proportional (*verhältnismäßig*) to the protection of health (BVerfG, Decision 1 BvR 971/21-, Rn. 1-222).

CONCLUDING REMARKS

Governments act under unbearable pressure in emergencies, but they count on legal instruments that, otherwise, could not be used. The effects produced by the COVID-19 pandemic are deeper than those spawned by previous global crises.

Comparing the responses of the German and the Spanish governments since March 2020 through early 2022 throws instructive results about their distinct understandings of emergency rule. This chapter has argued that they draw on constitutional, political, and parliamentary factors.

The German constitutional culture bears the stamp of the Weimar experience; the current constitutional provisions on emergency powers rely on that most determining influence to the point of largely explaining the choice of ordinary laws over emergency rule in facing the pandemic. Some seven decades of institution-building have created in the political class and the public a widespread trust in the constitutional resourcefulness of ordinary laws. In Spain, by contrast, the experience of the Second Republic and its emergency legislation, even if periodically remembered in scholarly and public debates, plays a less perceptible role in the constitutional culture. There was no appreciable controversiality in the Spanish government's choice of emergency rule in 2020, apart from scholars and journalists' warnings criticising a political decision that twice found ample parliamentary endorsement.

Across the pandemic's successive waves, each government has changed its way of ruling (from cooperative to more centralised the German, from centralised to decentralised the Spanish) in response, apart from public opinion concerns, to criticisms by minister presidents and by regional premiers, respectively. In other words, throughout the pandemic, the cooperation between federal and *Länder* governments in Germany has gone in the opposite direction than the one described in Spain between the executive and the governments of autonomous communities. In office in both countries were coalition governments, yet backed by unequal assets: the German ones were rooted in a long history of grand-coalitions, whereas the Spanish proved internally less stable and relied on more uncertain parliamentary support.

Furthermore, the COVID-19 response has not been just a matter of approaching a public health crisis. It tells something about ruling that in normal politics is missing, or dormant, which relates to parliamentary culture. Having both countries a lengthy parliamentary history, the role of parliament in the pandemic has been quite different. Whereas the activities of the *Bundestag* have followed their normal course (Bolleyer & Salát, 2021), the Congress of Deputies has remained for months almost an idle parliament. The performance of a democratic regime is measured, among other benchmarks, by the vitality of its parliament. In this regard, the Weimar lesson remains valid, namely, the longer the recourse to emergency rule, the more difficult becomes to get back to the normal functioning of a constitutional democracy.

NOTES

1. For reasons that become apparent in this chapter, translations of German and Spanish terms and quotes are mine; they do not always match those of official or of widely circulated English versions.
2. See https://www.boe.es.

ACKNOWLEDGEMENTS

Earlier versions of this chapter have been presented at workshops funded by COST Action 16211 *Reappraising Intellectual Debates on Civic Rights and Democracy in Europe* (RECAST, Horizon 2020 Framework Programme) and *Civic Constellation III: Democracy, Constitutionalism, and Antiliberalism* project (Spain's Research Fund, PGC2018-093573-B-I00). I have learnt much from their lively discussions. Later, the chapter has greatly benefitted from *Studies*' reviews.

REFERENCES

Aragón, M. (2020, April 10). Hay que tomarse la Constitución en serio. *El País*. https://elpais.com/elpais/2020/04/09/opinion/1586420090_736317.html

Ballbé, M. (1983). *Orden público y militarismo en la España constitucional (1812–1983)*. Alianza.

Bjork, J., & Spohr, K. (Eds.). (2016). Forum: Paul Preston's *The Spanish Holocaust* and recent historiography on the Spanish Second Republic. *Journal of Contemporary History*, 52(1), 412–438.

Bolleyer, N., & Salát, O. (2021). Parliaments in times of crisis: COVID-19, populism and executive dominance. *West European Politics*, 44(5–6), 1103–1128.

Bundesverfassungsgestz (B-VG) (Austrian Constitution of 1920). Gesetz vom 1. Oktober 1920, womit die Republik Österreich als Bundesstaat eingerichtet wird, BGBl. Nr. 1/1920. https://www.ris.bka.gv.at/GeltendeFassung.wxe?Abfrage=Bundesnormen&Gesetzesnummer=10000041&FassungVom=1920-12-01

Cacho, J. (2020, April 19). Gravedad extrema, decisiones heroicas. *Vozpópuli*. https://www.vozpopuli.com/opinion/decisiones-heroicas-casado-sanchez-jesus-cacho_0_1347165791.html

Cebada Romero, A., & Domínguez Redondo, E. (2021, February 26). *Spain: One pandemic and two versions of the state of alarm*. Verfassungsblog. https://verfassungsblog.de/spain-one-pandemic-and-two-versions-of-the-state-of-alarm

COVID-19 Civic Freedom Tracker. (2022). International Center for Not-For-Profit Law. https://www.icnl.org/covid19tracker/

DSCCRE: Diary of Sessions of the Constituent Parliament of the Spanish Republic (Diario de Sesiones de las Cortes Constituyentes de la República Española). (1931). https://app.congreso.es/est_sesiones

Dyzenhaus, D. (2012). States of emergency. In M. Rosenfeld & A. Sajó (Eds.), *The Oxford handbook of comparative constitutional law* (pp. 442–462). Oxford University Press.

The Economist. (2020, October 3). *Spain's poisonous politics have worsened the pandemic and the economy*. https://www.economist.com/europe/2020/10/03/spains-poisonous-politics-have-worsened-the-pandemic-and-the-economy

European Commission. (2021). *Recovery plan for Europe (NextGenerationEU)*. https://ec.europa.eu/info/strategy/recovery-plan-europe_en

Goetz, K. H., & Martinsen, D. S. (2021). COVID-19: A dual challenge to European liberal democracy. *West European Politics*, 44(5–6), 1003–1024.

Grau, R. (1922). *Die Diktaturgewalt des Reichspräsidenten und der Landesregierungen auf Grund des Artikel 48 der Reichsverfassung*. Otto Liebmann.

Haffner, S. (2018 [1979]). *Die deutsche Revolution, 1918/19*. Rowohlt.

Khakee, A. (2009). *Securing democracy? A comparative analysis of emergency powers in Europe* [Policy paper 30]. Geneva Centre for the Democratic Control of Armed Forces. https://www.files.ethz.ch/isn/99550/PP30_Anna_Khakee_Emergency_Powers.pdf

Kirschheimer, O. (2017 [1930a]). Artikel 48 – der falsche Weg. In H. Buchstein (Ed.), *Gesammelte Schriften, vol. 1: Recht und Politik in der Weimarer Republik* (pp. 349–353). Nomos.

Kirschheimer, O. (2017 [1930b]). Artikel 48 und die Wandlungen des Verfassungssystems. Auch ein Beitrag zum Verffassungstag. In H. Buchstein (Ed.), *Gesammelte Schriften, vol. 1: Recht und Politik in der Weimarer Republik* (pp. 202–205). Nomos.

Kolb, E., & Schumann, D. (2013). *Die Weimarer Republik* (8th ed.). Oldenbourg.

Lindseth, P. L. (2004). The paradox of parliamentary supremacy: Delegation, democracy, and dictatorship in Germany and France, 1920–1950s. *The Yale Law Journal, 113*, 1341–1415.
McIlwain, C. H. (1947). *Constitutionalism: Ancient and modern* (rev. ed.). Cornell University Press.
Möller, H. (2008). *Die Weimarer Republik. Eine unvollendete Demokratie* (9th ed.). Deutscher Taschenbuch Verlag.
Mommsen, H. (2009). *Aufstieg und Untergang der Republik von Weimar, 1918–1933* (3rd ed.). Ullstein.
Özbudun, E., & Turhan, M. (1995). *Emergency powers*. European Commission for Democracy Through Law, CDL-STD(1995)012. https://www.venice.coe.int/webforms/documents/?pdf=CDL-STD(1995)012-e
Prego, V. (2020, August 26). Unas cuantas falsedades envueltas en una dejación de responsabilidad. *El Independiente*. https://www.elindependiente.com/opinion/2020/08/26/unas-cuantas-falsedades-envueltas-en-una-dejacion-de-responsabilidad
Presidencia del Gobierno (Head of Government's Office). (2020, April 28). *Plan de desescalada*. https://www.lamoncloa.gob.es/consejodeministros/Paginas/enlaces/280420-enlace-desescalada.aspx
Presno Linera, M. Á., & García Majado, P. (2021, July 28). *A brief comment on the Spanish Constitutional Court Judgment concerning the first COVID-19 state of alarm*. Lex-Atlas: COVID-19. https://lexatlas-c19.org/a-brief-comment-on-the-spanish-constitutional-court-judgment-concerning-the-first-COVID-19-state-of-alarm/
Preuß, H. (2008 [1925]). Die Bedeutung des Artikels 48 der Reichsverfassung. In *Gesammelte Schriften, vol. 4: Politik und Verfassung in der Weimarer Republik* (edited and introduced by D. Lehnert, pp. 571–575). Mohr Siebeck.
Reichstagswahlen in Deutschland. (2021). *Wikipedia*. Retrieved January 4, 2022, from https://de.wikipedia.org/wiki/Reichstagswahlen_in_Deutschland
Respuesta del Gobierno. (2020, September 18). *Respuesta del Gobierno a pregunta escrita (184)*. Congreso de los Diputados. https://www.congreso.es/entradap/l14p/e5/e_0055549_n_000.pdf
Reusken C. B. E. M., Broberg, E. K., Haagmans, B., Meijer, A., Corman, V. M., Papa, A., Charrel, R., Drosten, C., Koopmans, M., Leitmeyer, K., & on behalf of EVD-LabNet and ERLI-Net. (2020, February 13). Laboratory readiness and response for novel coronavirus (2019-nCoV) in expert laboratories in 30 EU/EEA countries, January 2020. *Eurosurveillance, 25*(6), pii=2000082. https://doi.org/10.2807/1560-7917.ES.2020.25.6.2000082
Rössler, H.-C. (2020, October 14). Spanien hat die Kontrolle verloren. *Frankfurter Allgemeine Zeitung*. https://www.faz.net/aktuell/politik/ausland/corona-krise-spanien-hat-die-kontrolle-verloren-17000344.html
Schmitt, C. (2009 [1922]). *Politische Theologie. Vier Kapitel zur Lehre von der Souveränität* (9th ed.). Duncker & Humblot.
Schmitt, C. (2003 [1928]). *Verfassungslehre* (10th ed.). Duncker & Humblot.
Sell, F. L. (2020, October 9). Ist Spanien ein "failed state" – und wie soll die EU mit seinem Mitglied umgehen? *Neue Zürcher Zeitung*. https://www.nzz.ch/meinung/eine-eu-finanzhilfe-fuer-spanien-ist-derzeit-nicht-verantwortbar-ld.1579042
Steffen, T. (2021, April 21). Wie das neue Gesetz in den Alltag eingreift. *Die Zeit*. https://www.zeit.de/politik/deutschland/2021-04/infektionsschutzgesetz-coronavirus-notbremse-ausgangssperre-bundestag-faq
Varela, I. (2020, April 24). Orden en el país, caos en el Gobierno. *El Confidencial*. https://blogs.elconfidencial.com/espana/una-cierta-mirada/2020-04-24/coronavirus-orden-pais-caos-gobierno_2563895
Venice Commission. (2022). *Observatory on emergency situations*. https://www.venice.coe.int/files/EmergencyPowersObservatory//T09-E.htm
Weber, M. (1988 [1917]). Parlament und Regierung in neugeordneten Deutschland. In W. J. Mommsen (Ed.), *Studienausgabe der Max Weber-Gesamtausgabe, vol. I/15: Zur Politik im Weltkrieg. Schriften und Reden 1914–1918* (pp. 202–302). J.C.B. Mohr (Paul Siebeck).
Wissenschaftliche Dienste des Deutschen Bundestages. (2014, March 5). *Ermächtigungsgesetze von 1914 bis 1933 und die SPD* (WD 1–3000 – 015/14). https://www.bundestag.de/resource/blob/407790/73e315cf2696714d2451d7d4edf67519/WD-1-015-14-pdf-data.pdf
Wissenschaftliche Dienste des Deutschen Bundestages. (2020, April 22). *Koordinierung der Maßnahmen zur Eindämmung des Coronavirus durch die Bundesregierung* (WD 3 – 3000 – 105/20). https://www.bundestag.de/resource/blob/692490/5883cb39172f495b6044317360e67a00/WD-3-105-20-pdf-data.pdf

Wissenschaftliche Dienste des Deutschen Bundestages. (2021, February 8). *Bund-Länder-Konferenzen zur Corona-Pandemie* (WD 3 – 3000 – 031/21). https://www.bundestag.de/resource/blob/828932/f901ae2c63048b60a12b1839928d6688/WD-3-031-21-pdf-data.pdf

World Health Organization. (2020, January 30). *Statement on the second meeting of the International Health Regulations (2005) Emergency Committee regarding the outbreak on novel Coronavirus (2919-nCoV)*. https://www.who.int/news-room/detail/30-01-2020-statement-on-the-second-meeting-of-the-international-health-regulations-(2005)-emergency-committee-regarding-the-outbreak-of-novel-coronavirus-(2019-ncov)

GERMAN LEGAL DOCUMENTS

Bundesverfassungsgericht (BVerfG) (Federal Constitutional Court), Beschluss des Ersten Senats, vom 19. November 2021 – 1 BvR 971/21-, Rn. 1-222. https://www.bundesverfassungsgericht.de/e/rs20211119_1bvr097121.html

Deutscher Bundestag. (2021, April 21). *Bevölkerungsschutzgesetz: Bundesweite Notbremse beschlossen.* https://www.bundestag.de/dokumente/textarchiv/2021/kw16-de-infektionsschutzgesetz-834802

Gesetz zur Behebung der Not von Volk und Reich (Ermächtigungsgesetz) (Enabling Act) (1933, March 24). http://www.verfassungen.de/de33-45/ermaechtigungsgesetz33.htm

Gesetz zum Schutze der Republik ([First] Law for the Protection of the Republic), July 21, 1922 (Reichgesetzblatt 1922 I, 585–90). http://www.documentarchiv.de/wr/repschutz_ges01.html

Gesetz zum Schutze der Republik ([Second] Law for the Protection of the Republic), March 25, 1930 (Reichgesetzblatt 1930 I, 91–3). http://www.documentarchiv.de/wr/1930/republikschutzgesetz.html

Gesetz zur Verhütung und Bekämpfung von Infektionskrankheiten beim Menschen (Infektionsschutzgesetz) (Infection Protection Act), vom 20. Juli 2000 (BGBl. I S. 1045), das zuletzt durch Artikel 2 des Gesetzes vom 10. Dezember 2021 (BGBl. I S. 5162) geändert worden ist. https://www.gesetze-im-internet.de/ifsg

Grundgesetz (GG) (Basic Law), first version. (1949, May 23). http://www.documentarchiv.de/brd/1949/grundgesetz.html

Grundgesetz, Official English translation. (2022). https://www.gesetze-im-internet.de/englisch_gg/englisch_gg.pdf

Notstandsgesetze (Emergency Acts), Siebzehntes Gesetz zur Ergänzung des Grundgesetzes (1968, June 24). http://www.documentarchiv.de/brd/1968/grundgesetz-notstandsgesetze.html

Notverordnungen. (2004). *Notverordnungen (Artikel 48 Abs. 3 der Reichsverfassung), Verordnungen und Erlasse des Reichspresidenten.* http://www.documentarchiv.de/da/fs-notverordnungen_reichspraesident.html

Die Verfassung des Deutschen Reiches (Weimarer Reichsverfassung) (WVerf) (Weimar Constitution), August 11, 1919 (Reichsgesetzblatt 1919, S. 1383). https://www.jura.uni-wuerzburg.de/fileadmin/02160100/Elektronische_Texte/Verfassungstexte/Die_Weimarer_Reichsverfassung_2017ge.pdf

SPANISH LEGAL DOCUMENTS

Constitución de la República Española (CE 1931) (Spanish Constitution of 1931), December 9. https://www.congreso.es/docu/constituciones/1931/1931_cd.pdf

Constitución Española de 1978 (CE 1978) (Spanish Constitution of 1978), December 29. https://www.congreso.es/docu/constituciones/1978/1978_cd.pdf

Constitutional Court Ruling (Sentencia del Tribunal Constitucional) 148/2021, of July 14, 2021. https://www.boe.es/boe/dias/2021/07/31/pdfs/BOE-A-2021-13032.pdf

Constitutional Court Ruling (Sentencia del Tribunal Constitucional) 183/2021, of October 27, 2021. https://www.boe.es/boe/dias/2021/11/25/pdfs/BOE-A-2021-19512.pdf

Constitutional Court Ruling on Unconstitutionality Question CI. 6283-2020, of June 2, 2022. https://www.boe.es/boe/dias/2021/02/23/pdfs/BOE-A-2021-2763.pdf

DSCCRE: Diary of Sessions of the Constituent Parliament of the Spanish Republic (Diario de Sesiones de las Cortes Constituyentes de la República Española). (1931). https://app.congreso.es/est_sesiones

General Law of Health 14/1986, of April 25. https://www.boe.es/eli/es/l/1986/04/25/14
Law 2/2021, of March 29, of urgent measures of prevention, containment and coordination to face the health crisis caused by COVID-19). https://www.boe.es/eli/es/l/2021/03/29/2/con
Ley de Defensa de la República (LDR), October 22, 1931. https://www.boe.es/datos/pdfs/BOE/1931/295/A00420-00421.pdf
Ley de Orden Público (LOP), July 30, 1933. https://www.boe.es/datos/pdfs/BOE/1933/211/A00682-00690.pdf
Organic Law 4/1981, of June 1, of the states of alarm, exception and siege. https://www.boe.es/eli/es/lo/1981/06/01/4/con
Organic Law 3/1986, of April 14, of special measures in matters of public health). https://www.boe.es/eli/es/lo/1986/04/14/3
Resolution of 29 October 2020 of the Congress of Deputies ordering the publication of the Authorization agreement to extend the state of alarm declared by Royal Decree 926/2020, of 25 October, declaring the state of alarm to contain the spread of infections caused by SARS-CoV-2. https://www.boe.es/eli/es/res/2020/10/29/(1)
Royal Decree 463/2020, of March 14, declaring the state of alarm to manage the situation of health crisis caused by the COVID-19. https://www.boe.es/eli/es/rd/2020/03/14/463/con
Royal Decree 926/2020, of October 25, declaring the state of alarm to contain the spread of infections caused by SARS-CoV-2). https://www.boe.es/eli/es/rd/2020/10/25/926
Royal Decree 956/2020, of November 3, extending the state of alarm declared by Royal Decree 926/2020, of 25 October, declaring the state of alarm to contain the spread of infections caused by SARS-CoV-2). https://www.boe.es/eli/es/rd/2020/11/03/956

Printed and bound by CPI Group (UK) Ltd, Croydon, CR0 4YY